Order No. HLE90000209
ISBN 0-7119-6427-0

Exclusive Distributors:
Music Sales Limited
8/9 Frith Street, London W1V 5TZ, England.
Music Sales Pty Limited
120 Rothschild Avenue, Rosebery, NSW 2018, Australia.

Cover design by Pearce Marchbank, Studio Twenty, London
Printed in the USA

MOVIE GREATS

Your Guarantee of Quality
As publishers, we strive to produce every book to
the highest commercial standards.
This book has been carefully designed to minimise awkward
page turns and to make playing from it a real pleasure.
Throughout, the printing and binding have been planned
to ensure a sturdy, attractive publication which should
give years of enjoyment.
If your copy fails to meet our high standards,
please inform us and we will gladly replace it.

Music Sales' complete catalogue describes thousands of titles
and is available in full colour sections by subject, direct from
Music Sales Limited. Please state your areas of interest and
send a cheque/postal order for £1.50 for postage to:
Music Sales Limited, Newmarket Road, Bury St. Edmunds,
Suffolk IP33 3YB, England.

Visit the Internet Music Shop at
http//www.musicsales.co.uk

Hal Leonard Europe
Distributed by Music Sales

A HARD DAY'S NIGHT
A HARD DAY'S NIGHT
PAGE 20

A WHOLE NEW WORLD
ALADDIN
PAGE 56

BABY ELEPHANT WALK
HATARI!
PAGE 4

BEYOND THE BLUE HORIZON
MONTE CARLO
PAGE 10

BUTTONS AND BOWS
PALEFACE
PAGE 12

CAN YOU FEEL THE LOVE TONIGHT
THE LION KING
PAGE 7

CHIM CHIM CHER-EE
MARY POPPINS
PAGE 14

FORREST GUMP
MAIN TITLE (FEATHER THEME)
FORREST GUMP
PAGE 16

ISN'T IT ROMANTIC?
LOVE ME TONIGHT
PAGE 22

IT'S A GRAND NIGHT FOR SINGING
STATE FAIR
PAGE 24

IT'S EASY TO REMEMBER
MISSISSIPPI
PAGE 26

LOVER
LOVE ME TONIGHT
PAGE 32

MOON RIVER
BREAKFAST AT TIFFANY'S
PAGE 36

SOMEWHERE OUT THERE
AN AMERICAN TAIL
PAGE 40

TAKE MY BREATH AWAY (LOVE THEME)
TOP GUN
PAGE 46

THAT OLD BLACK MAGIC
STAR SPANGLED RHYTHM
PAGE 50

THE NEARNESS OF YOU
ROMANCE IN THE DARK
PAGE 38

THE RAINBOW CONNECTION
THE MUPPET MOVIE
PAGE 29

THE WAY YOU LOOK TONIGHT
SWING TIME
PAGE 54

UP WHERE WE BELONG
AN OFFICER AND A GENTLEMAN
PAGE 43

YOU SHOULD BE DANCING
SATURDAY NIGHT FEVER
PAGE 61

REGISTRATION GUIDE
PAGE 64

Baby Elephant Walk

from the Paramount Picture HATARI!

Registration 7
Rhythm: 8 Beat or Rock

By Henry Mancini

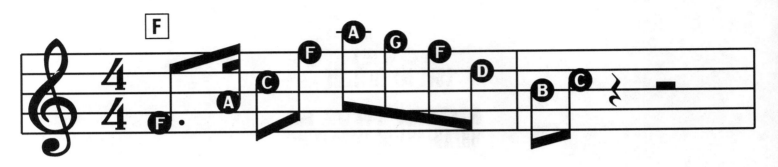

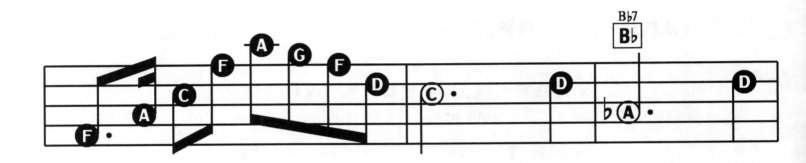

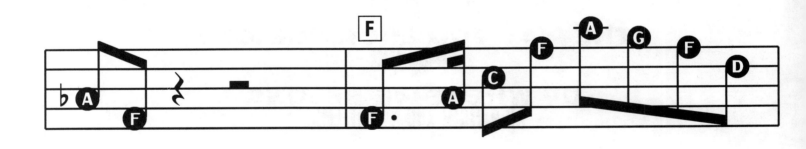

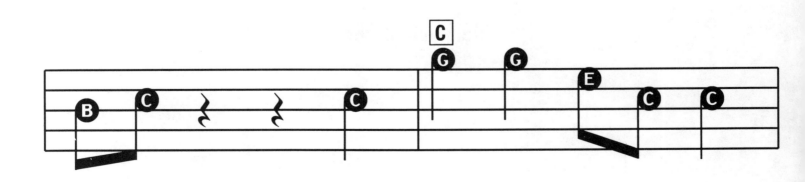

5

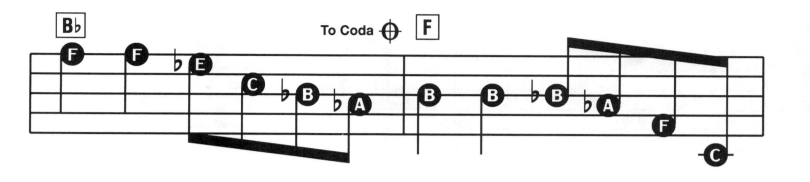

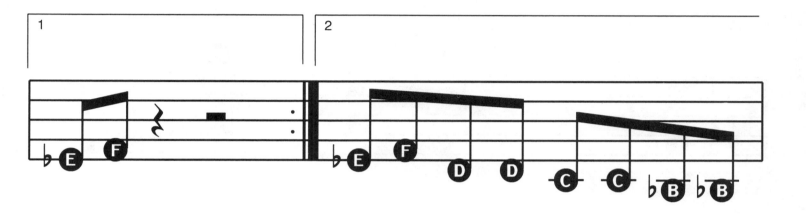

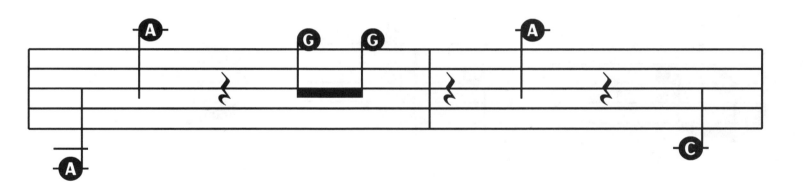

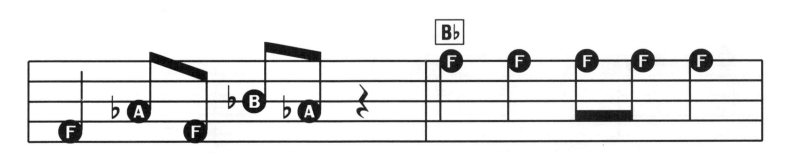

6

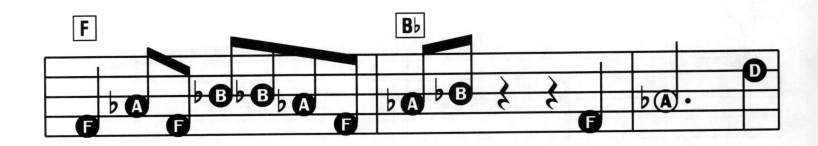

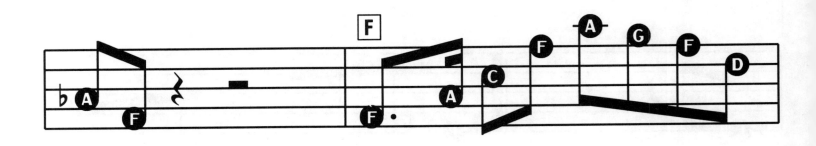

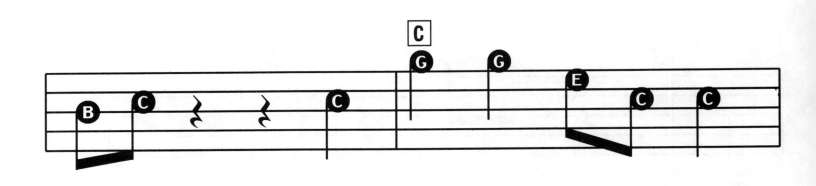

D.C. al Coda
(Return to beginning
Play to ⊕ and
Skip to Coda)

CODA
⊕

F7

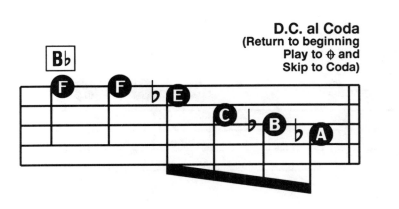

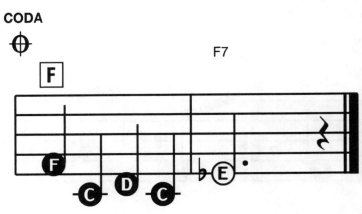

Can You Feel the Love Tonight
from Walt Disney Pictures' THE LION KING

Registration 2
Rhythm: Rock or 8 Beat

Music by Elton John
Lyrics by Tim Rice

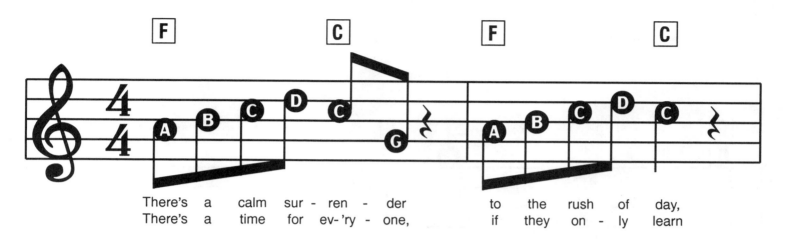

There's a calm sur - ren - der to the rush of day,
There's a time for ev - 'ry - one, if they on - ly learn

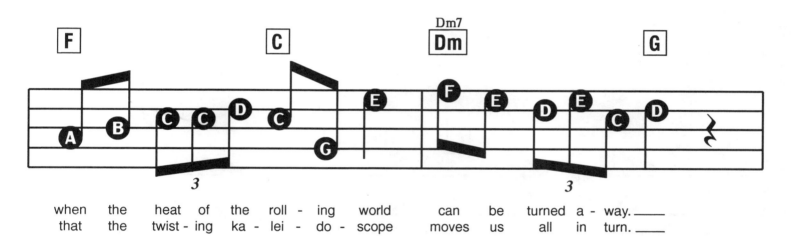

when the heat of the roll - ing world can be turned a - way. ___
that the twist - ing ka - lei - do - scope moves us all in turn. ___

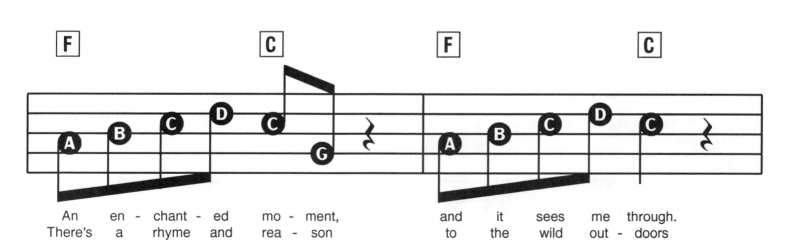

An en - chant - ed mo - ment, and it sees me through.
There's a rhyme and rea - son to the wild out - doors

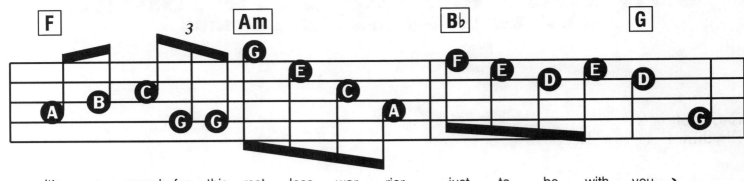

It's e-nough for this rest-less war-rior just to be with you. } And
when the heart of this star-crossed voy-ag-er beats in time with yours.

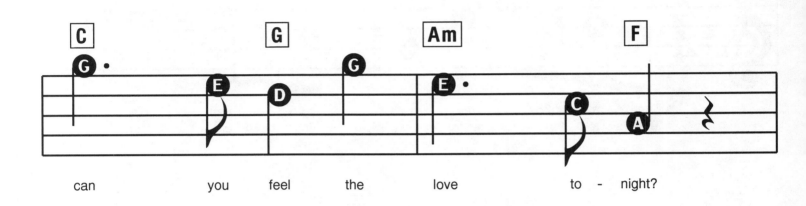

can you feel the love to - night?

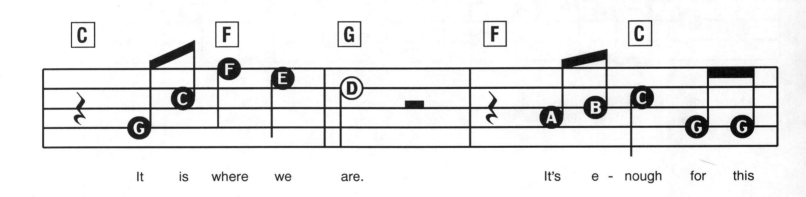

It is where we are. It's e - nough for this

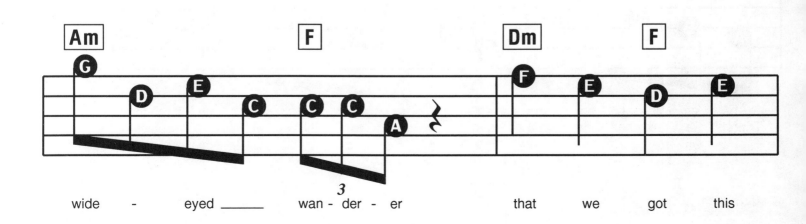

wide - eyed _____ wan - der - er that we got this

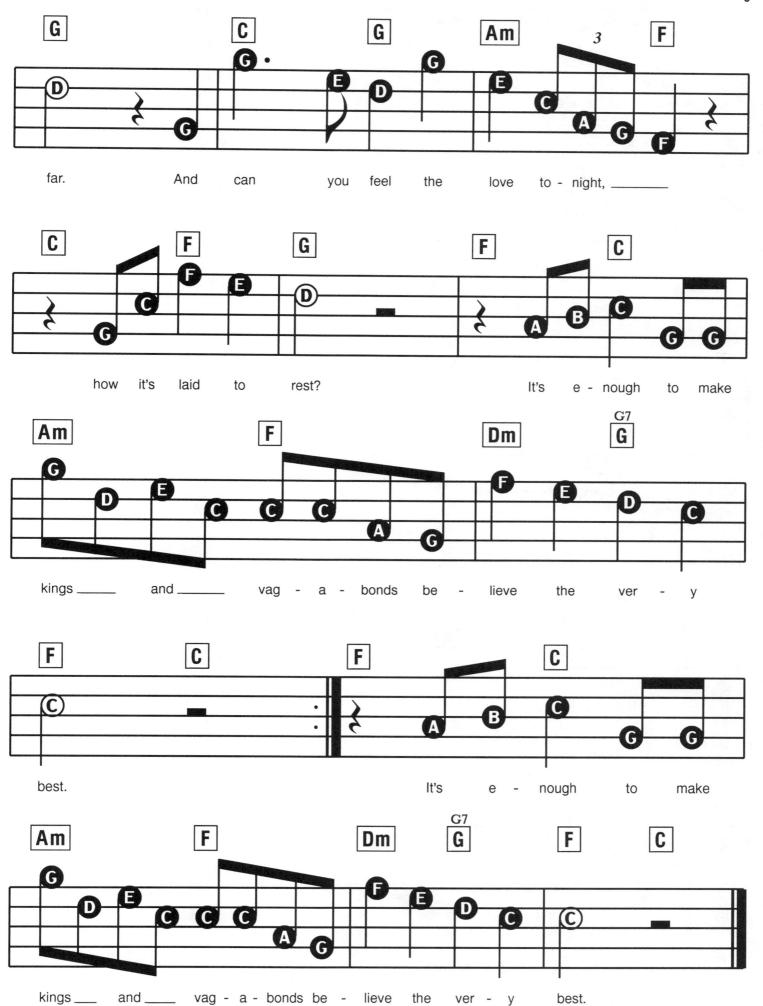

Beyond the Blue Horizon
from the Paramount Picture MONTE CARLO

Registration 3
Rhythm: Fox Trot or Rock

Words by Leo Robin
Music by Richard A. Whiting and W. Franke Harling

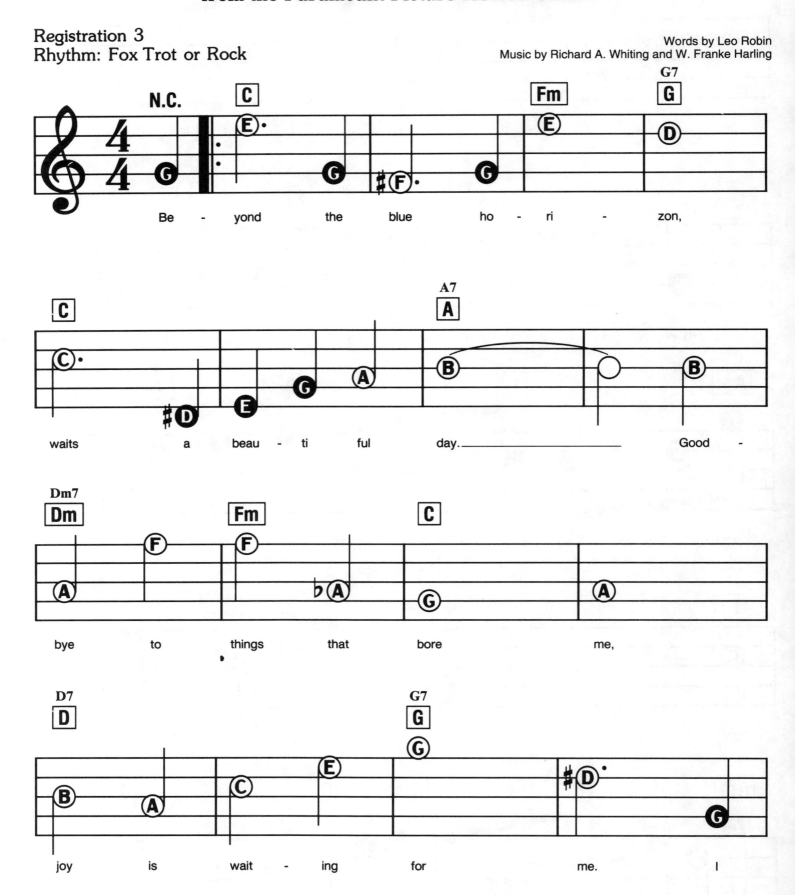

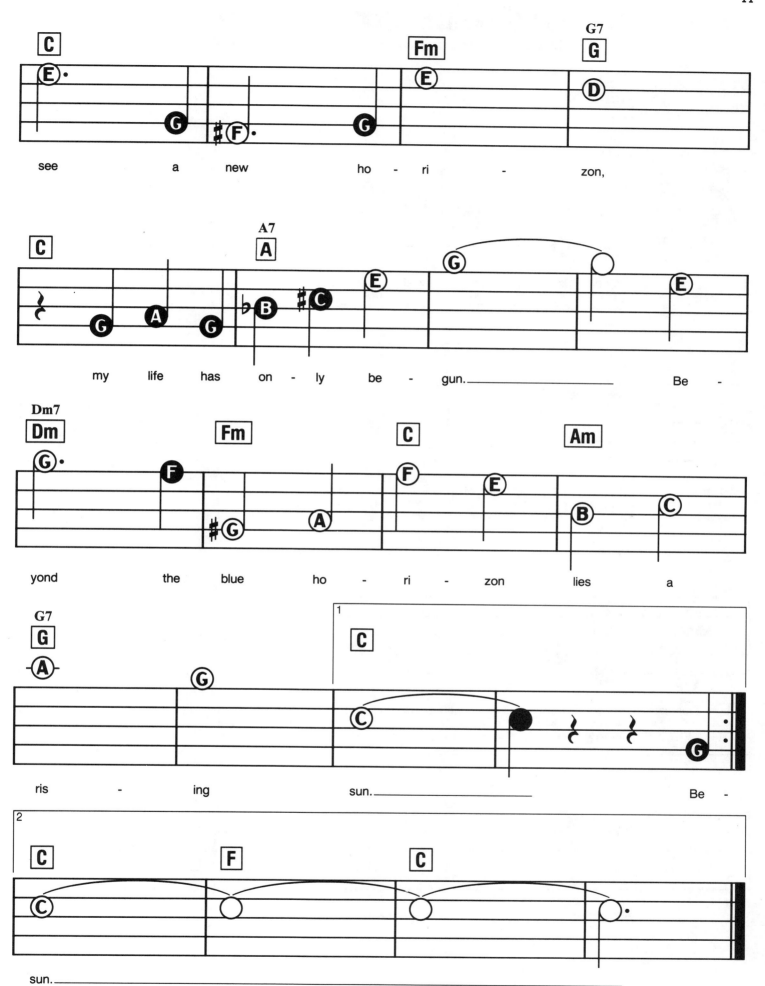

see a new ho - ri - zon,

my life has on - ly be - gun._____ Be -

yond the blue ho - ri - zon lies a

ris - ing sun._____ Be -

sun._____

Buttons and Bows
from the Paramount Picture PALEFACE

Registration 4
Rhythm: Swing

Words and Music by Jay Livingston
and Ray Evans

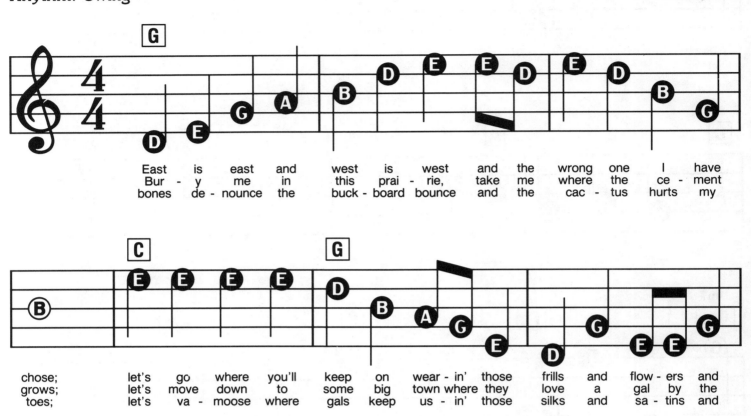

East is east and west is west and the wrong one I have
Bur - y me in this prai - rie, take me where the ce - ment
bones de - nounce the buck - board bounce and the cac - tus hurts my

chose; let's go where you'll keep on wear - in' those frills and flow - ers and
grows; let's move down to keep some big town where they love a gal by the
toes; let's va - moose where gals keep us - in' those silks and sa - tins and

but - tons and bows,_____ rings and things and but - tons and bows._____
cut of her clothes, and you'll stand out in but - tons and bows._____
lin - en that shows, and you're all mine in but - tons and bows._____

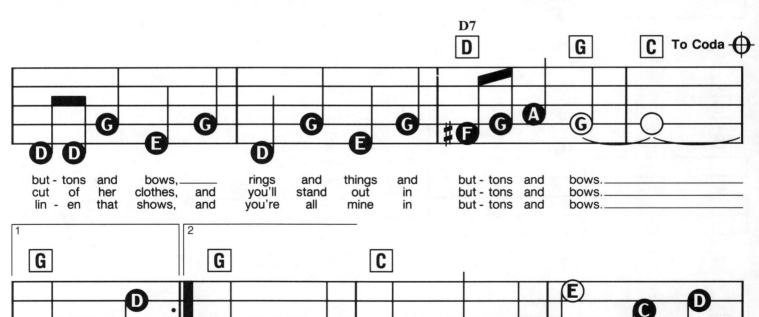

_____ Don't _____ I'll love you in buck - skin, or

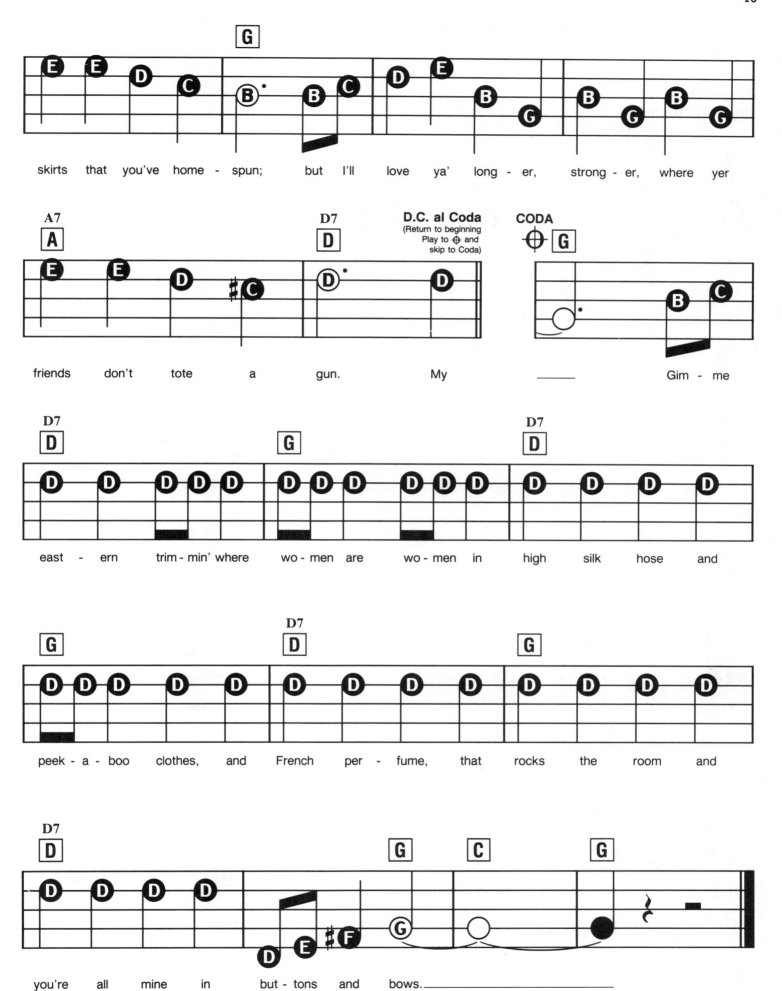

Chim Chim Cher-ee

from Walt Disney's MARY POPPINS

Registration 3
Rhythm: Waltz

Words and Music by
Richard M. Sherman and Robert B. Sherman

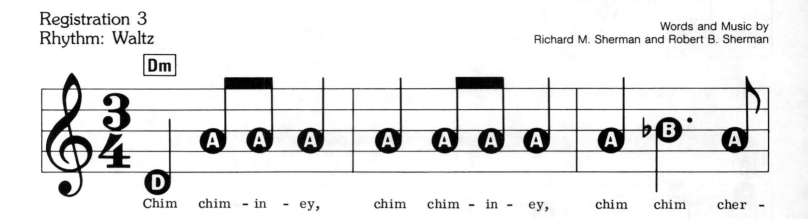

Chim chim - in - ey, chim chim - in - ey, chim chim cher -

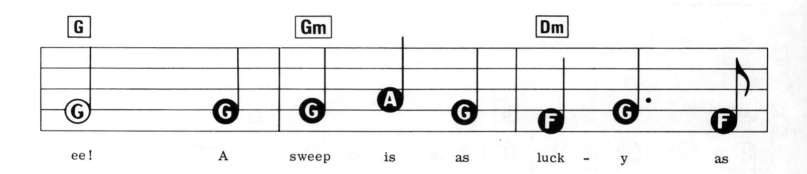

ee! A sweep is as luck - y as

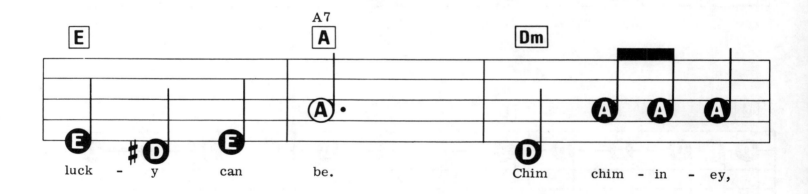

luck - y can be. Chim chim - in - ey,

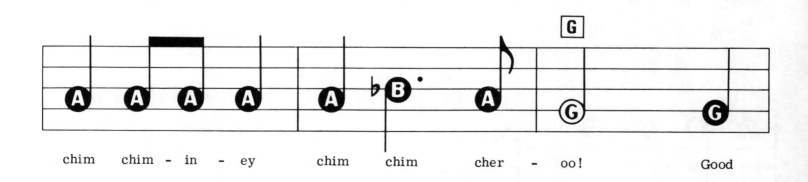

chim chim - in - ey chim chim cher - oo! Good

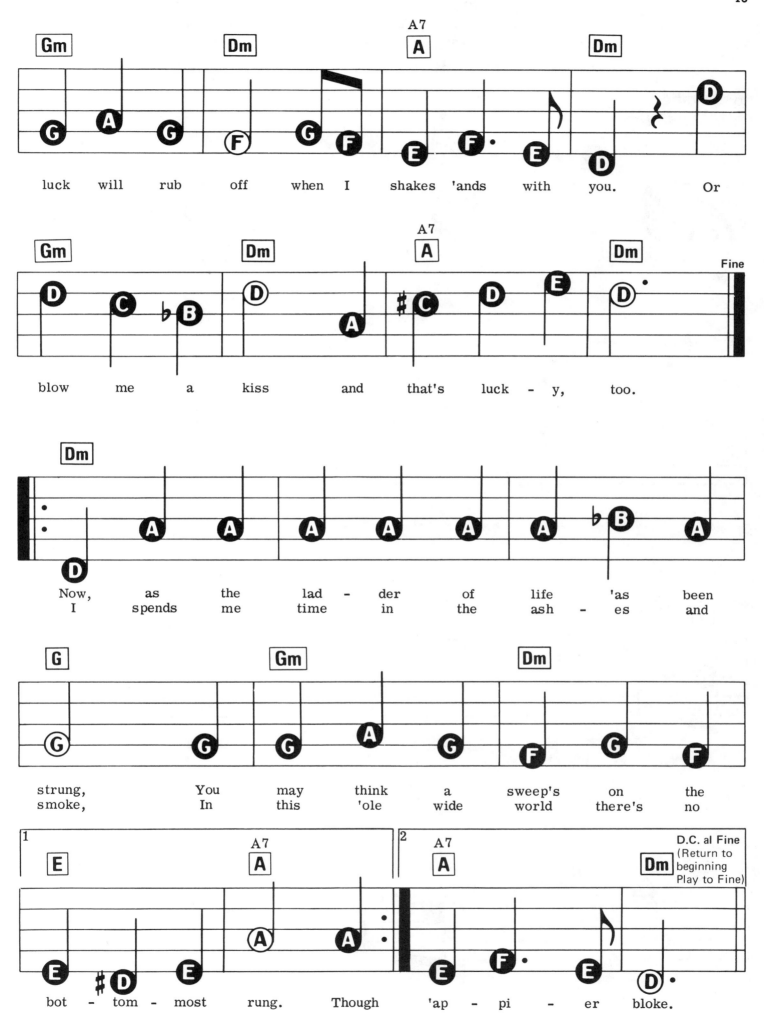

Forrest Gump - Main Title
(Feather Theme)
from the Paramount Motion Picture FORREST GUMP

Registration 8
Rhythm: Pop Rock

Music by Alan Silvestri

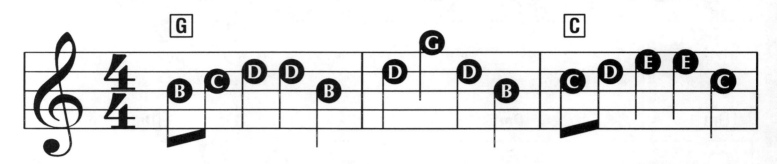

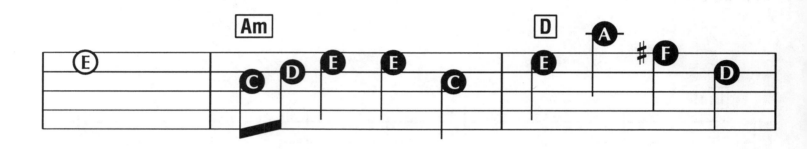

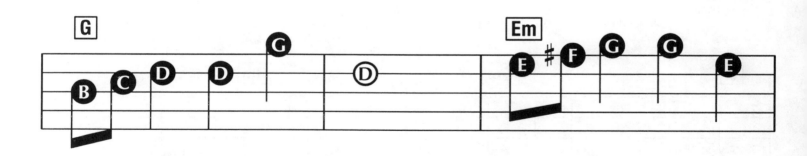

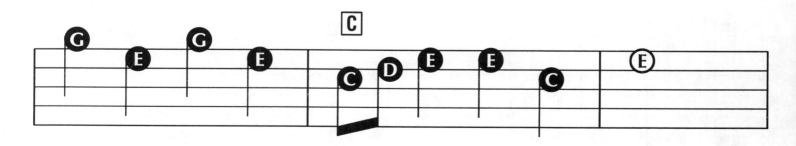

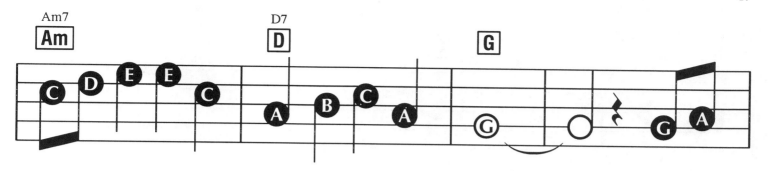

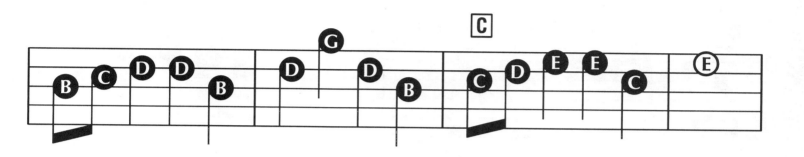

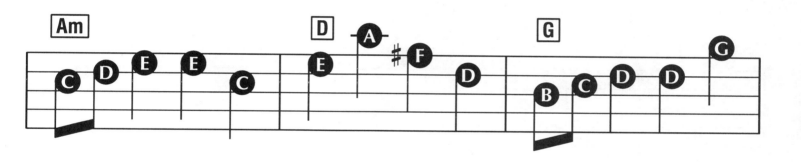

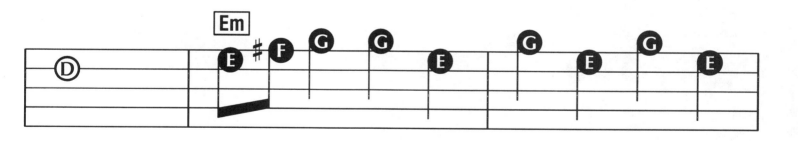

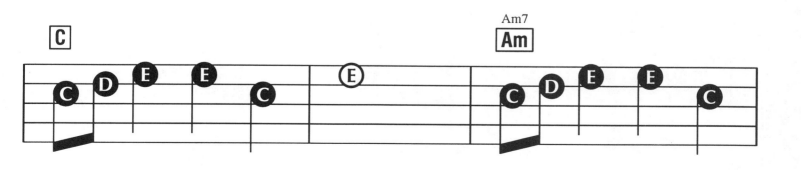

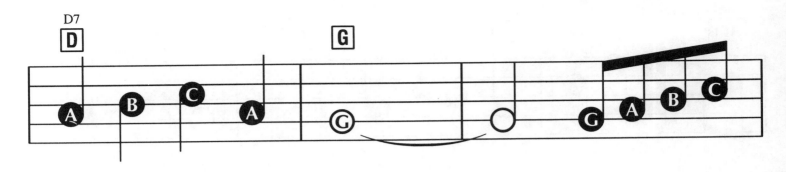

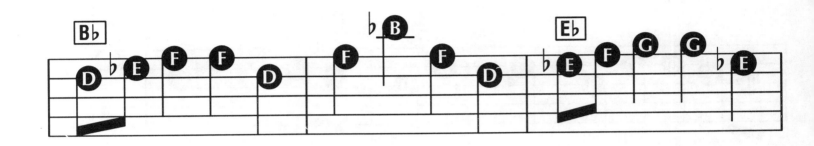

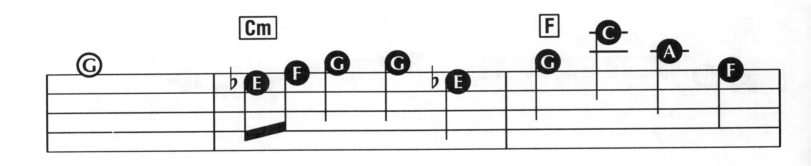

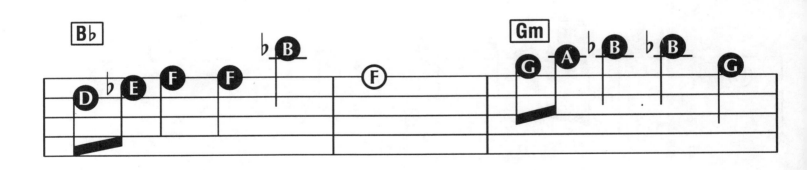

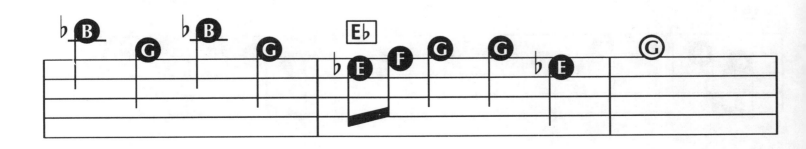

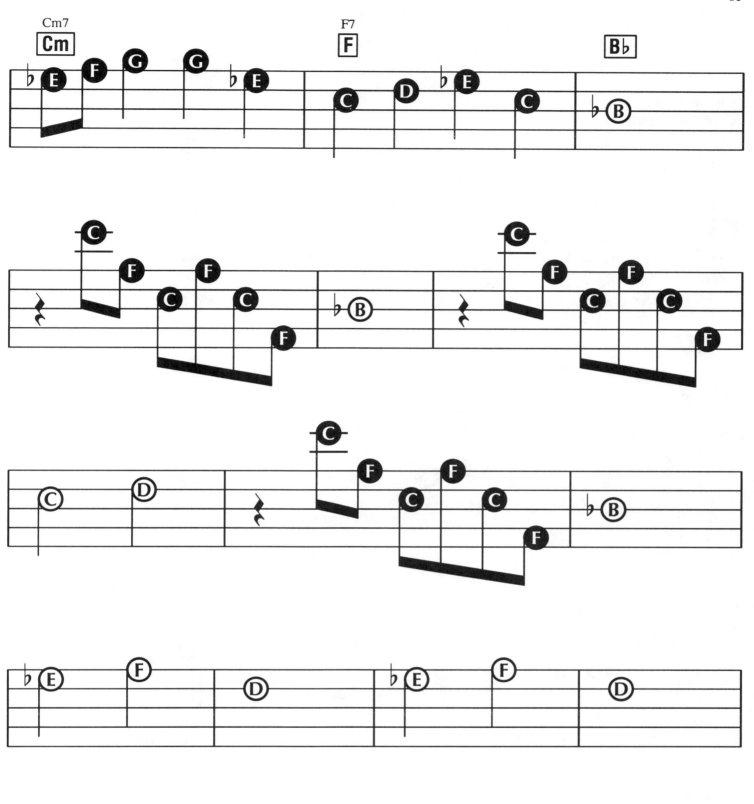
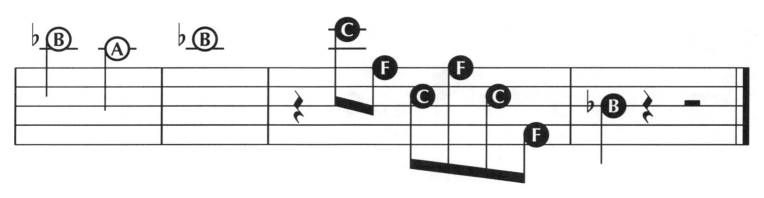

A Hard Day's Night

from A HARD DAY'S NIGHT

Registration 7
Rhythm: Rock

Words and Music by John Lennon
and Paul McCartney

Isn't It Romantic?
from the Paramount Picture LOVE ME TONIGHT

Words by Lorenz Hart
Music by Richard Rodgers

Registration 2
Rhythm: Swing or Big Band

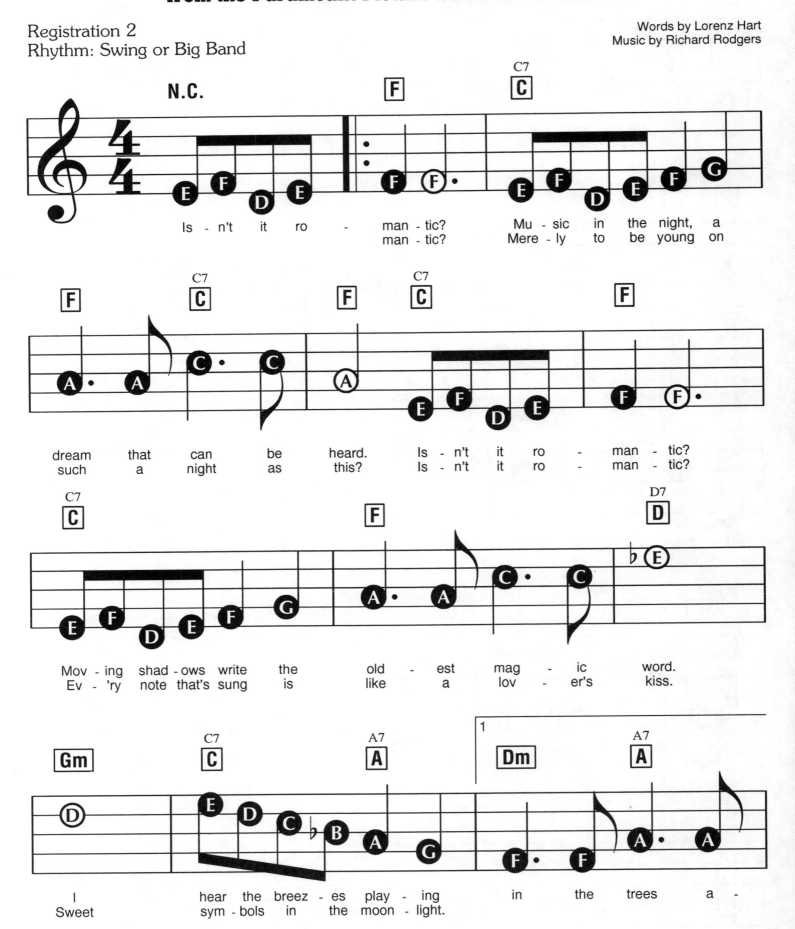

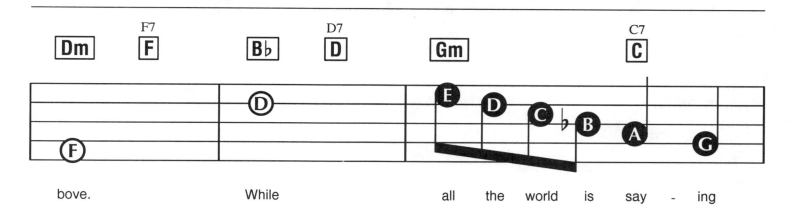

bove.   While   all   the   world   is   say - ing

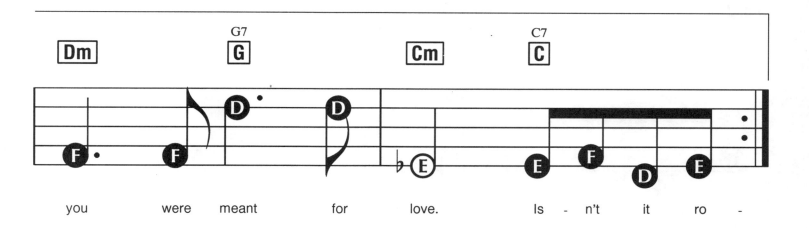

you   were   meant   for   love.   Is - n't   it   ro -

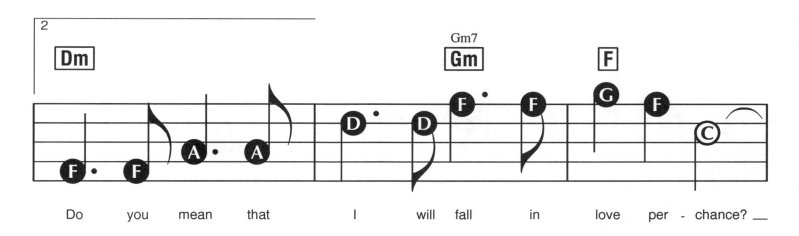

Do   you   mean   that   I   will   fall   in   love per - chance? __

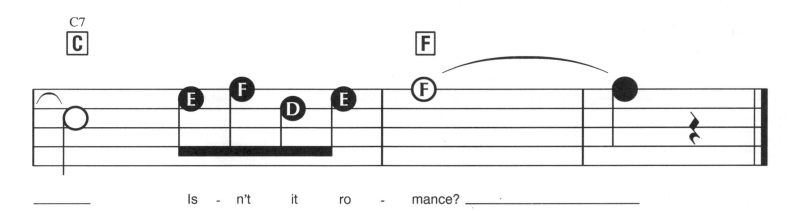

_____   Is - n't it ro - mance? _____

It's a Grand Night for Singing
from STATE FAIR

Registration 5
Rhythm: Waltz

Lyrics by Oscar Hammerstein II
Music by Richard Rodgers

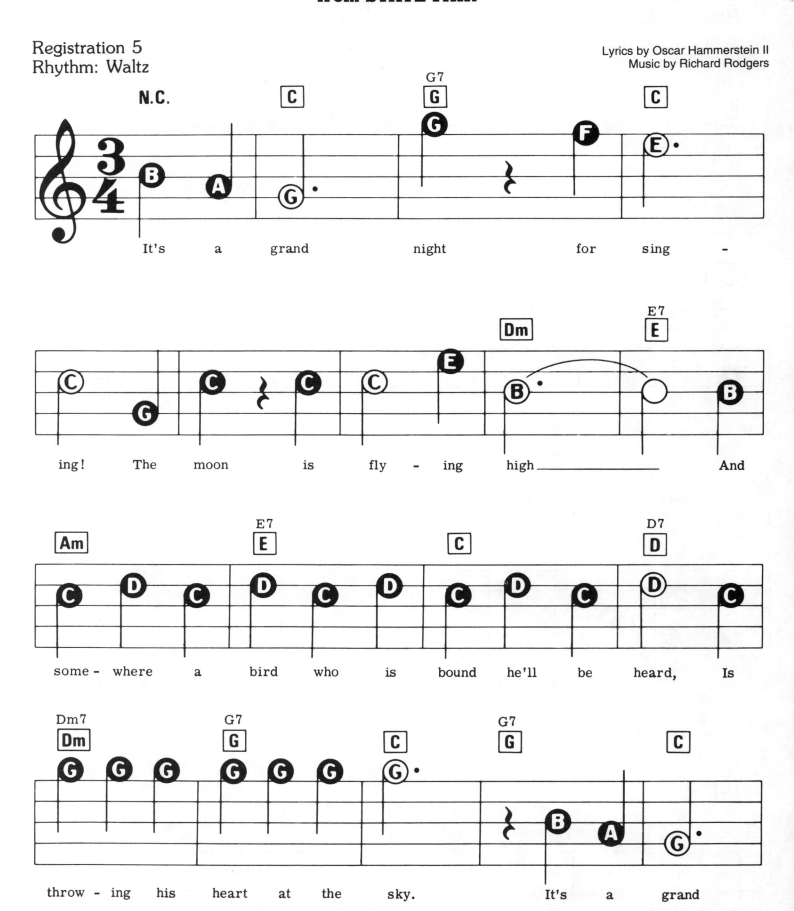

25

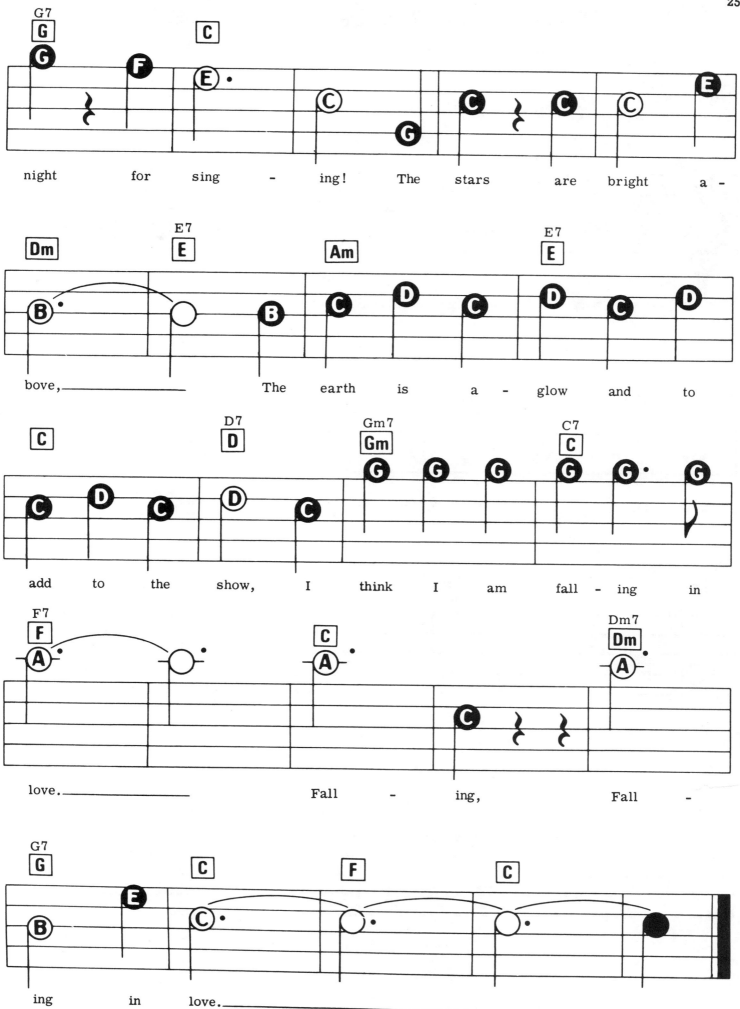

It's Easy to Remember

from the Paramount Picture MISSISSIPPI

Registration 7
Rhythm: Pops, Fox Trot or 8 Beat

Words by Lorenz Hart
Music by Richard Rodgers

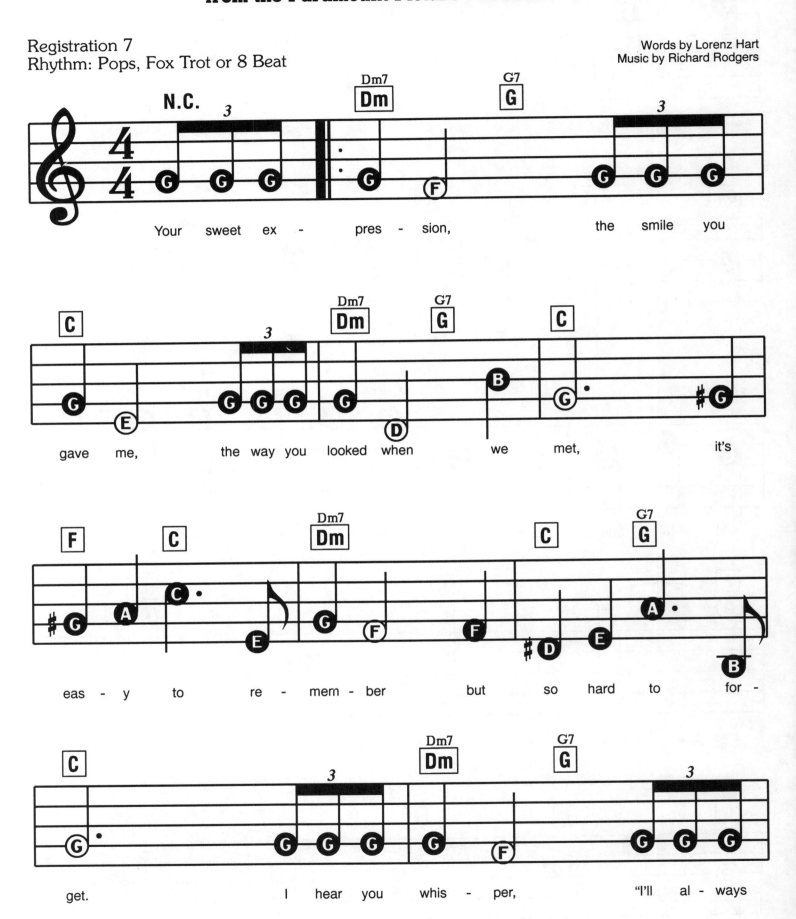

27

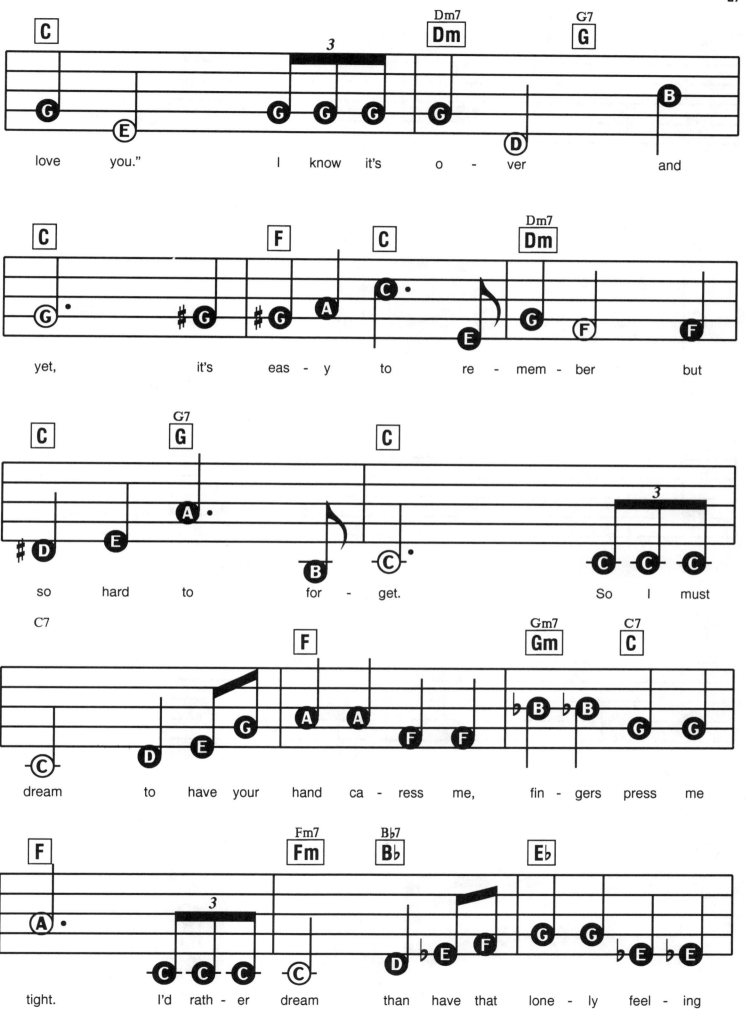

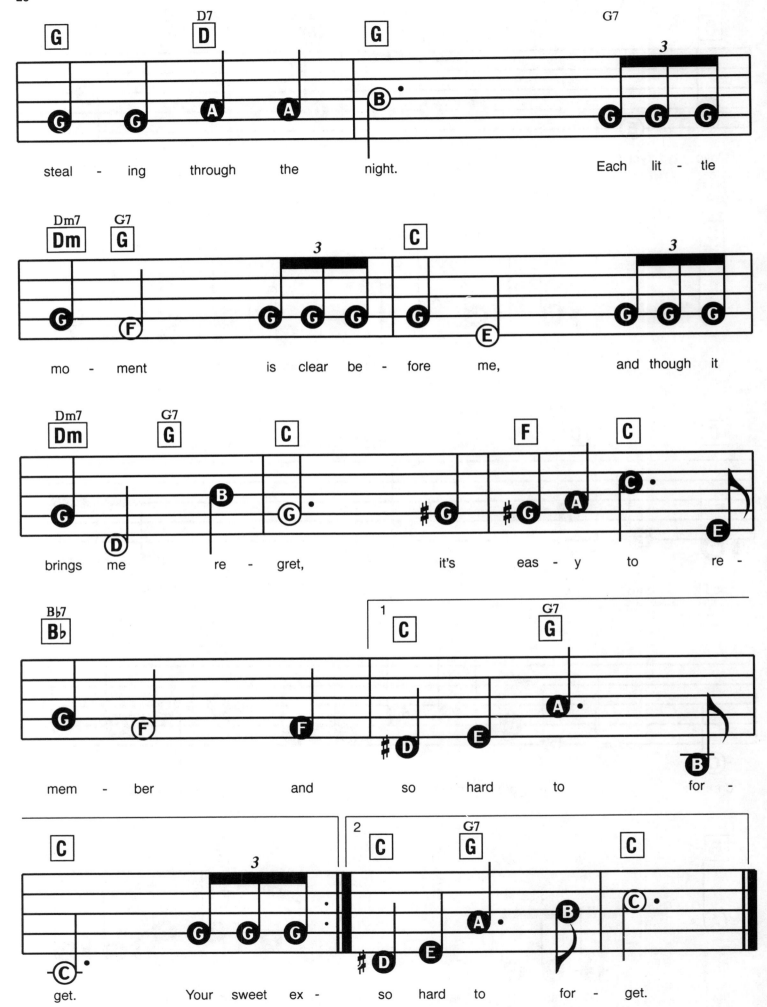

The Rainbow Connection
from THE MUPPET MOVIE

Registration 4
Rhythm: Waltz

By Paul Williams
and Kenneth L. Ascher

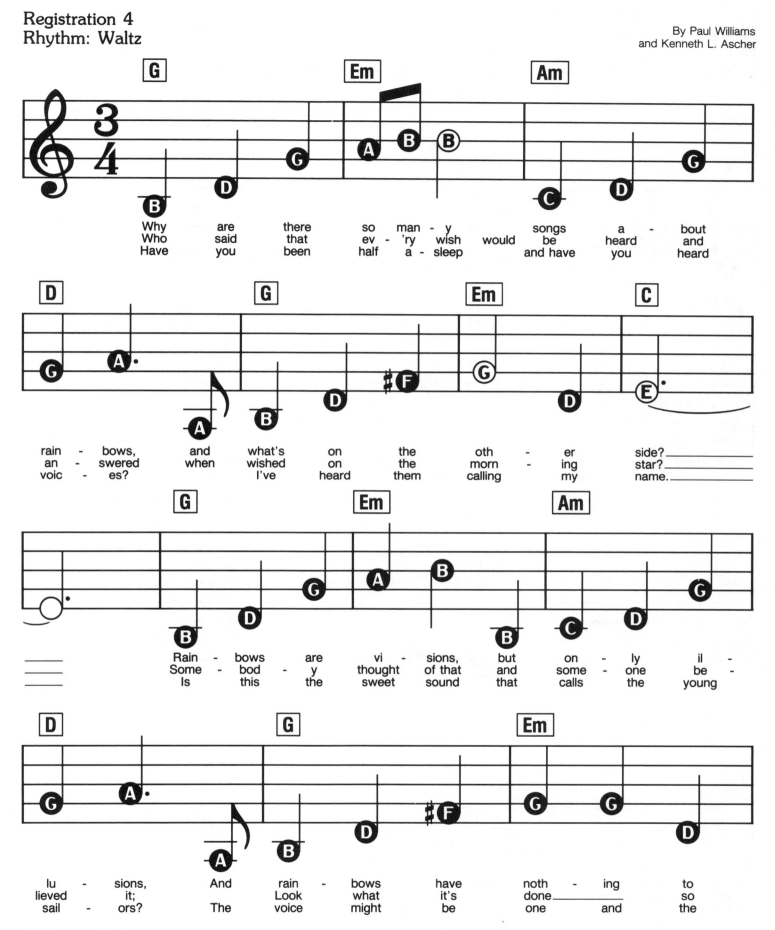

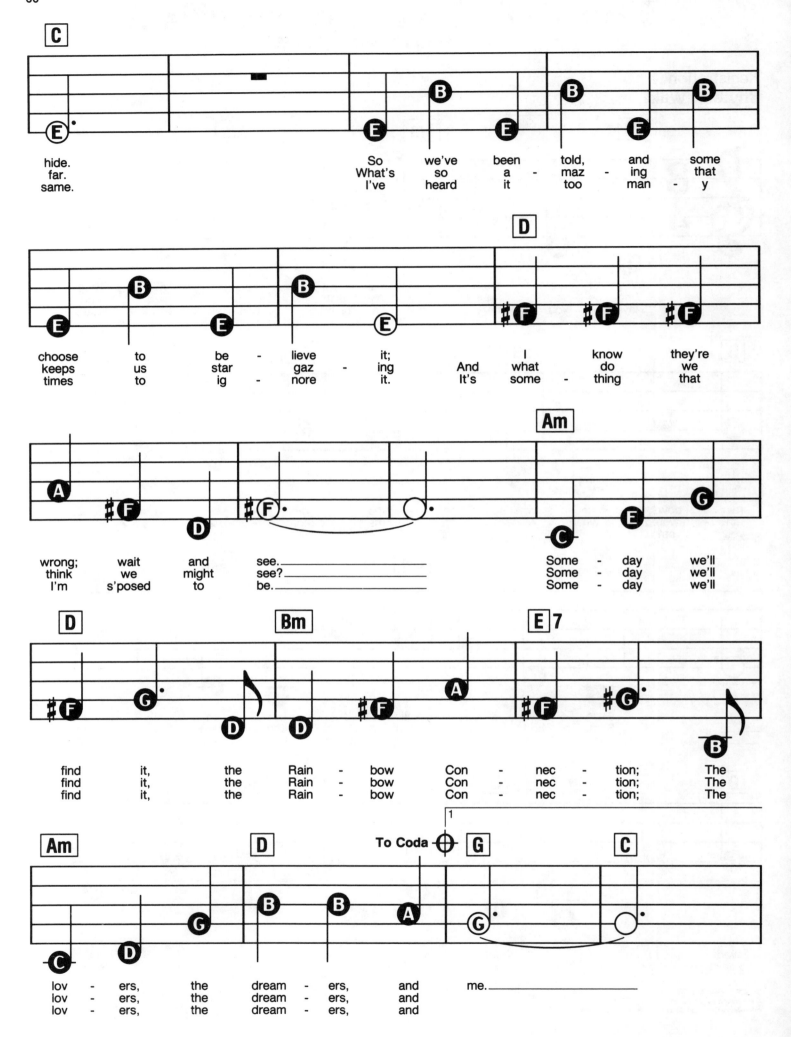

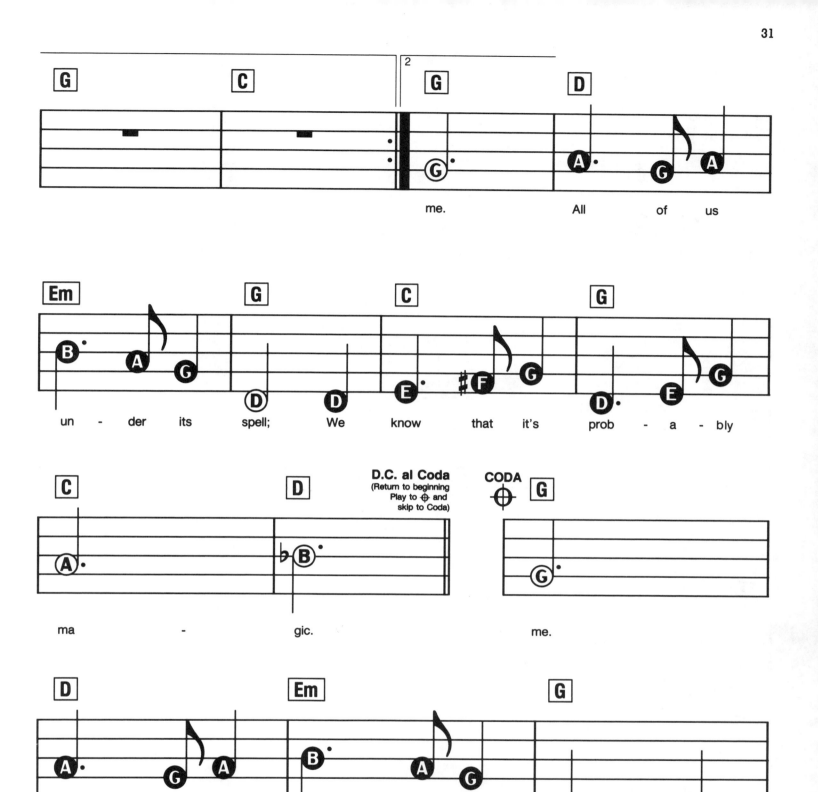

me.   All   of   us

un - der its   spell;   We   know   that   it's   prob - a - bly

D.C. al Coda
(Return to beginning
Play to ⊕ and
skip to Coda)

CODA

ma - gic.   me.

La   da   da   de   da   da   do   la

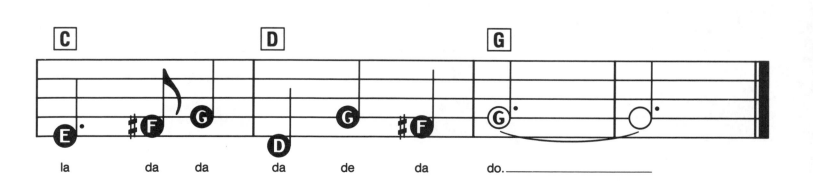

la   da   da   da   de   da   do.

Lover
from the Paramount Picture LOVE ME TONIGHT

Registration 6
Rhythm: Waltz

Lyric by Lorenz Hart
Music by Richard Rodgers

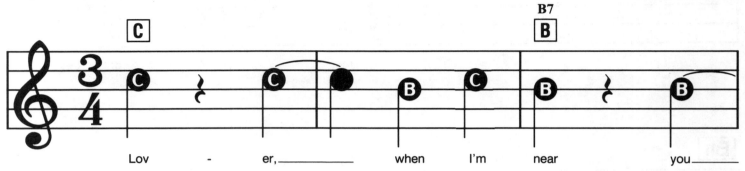

Lov - er,_____ when I'm near you_____

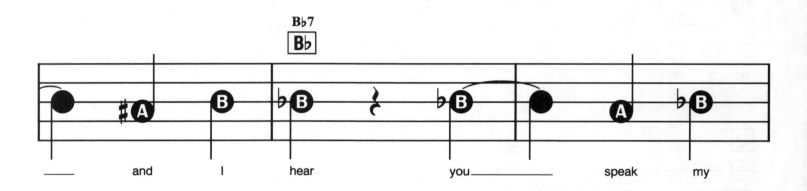

_____ and I hear you_____ speak my

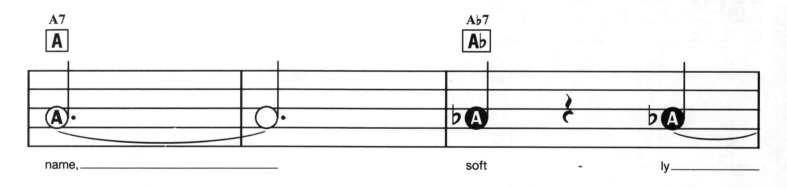

name,_____ soft - ly_____

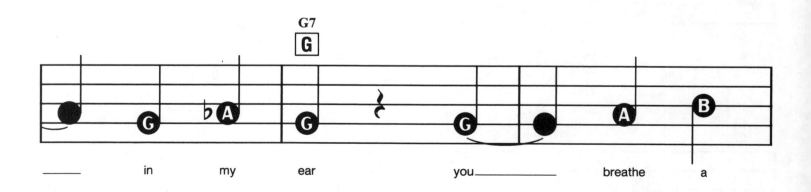

_____ in my ear you_____ breathe a

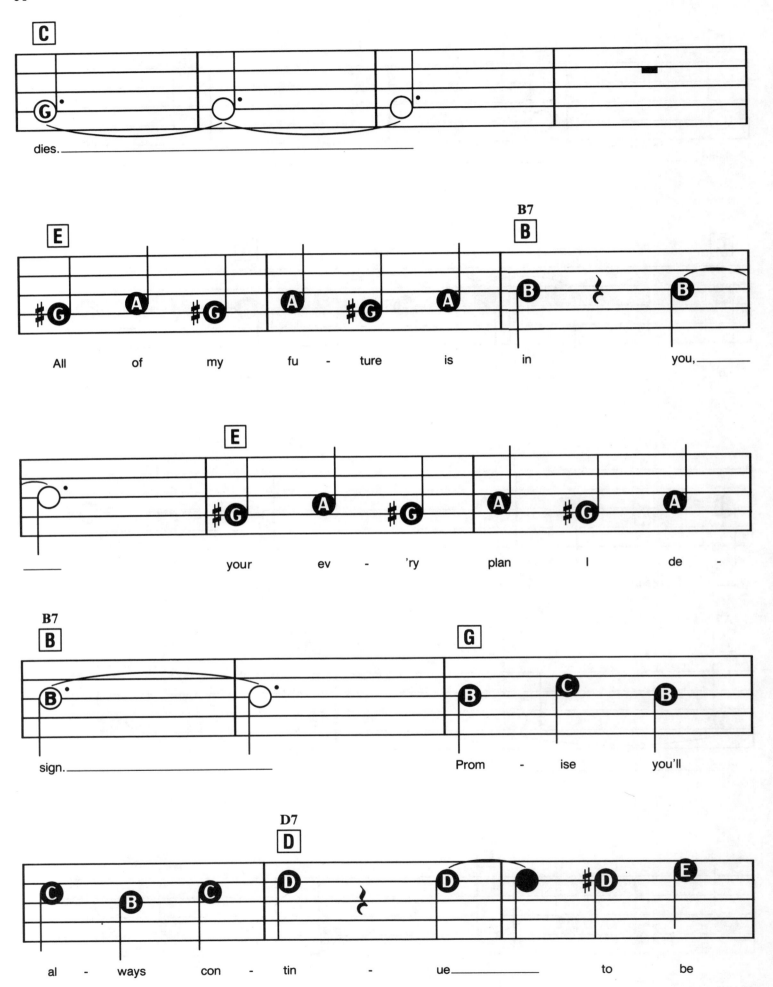

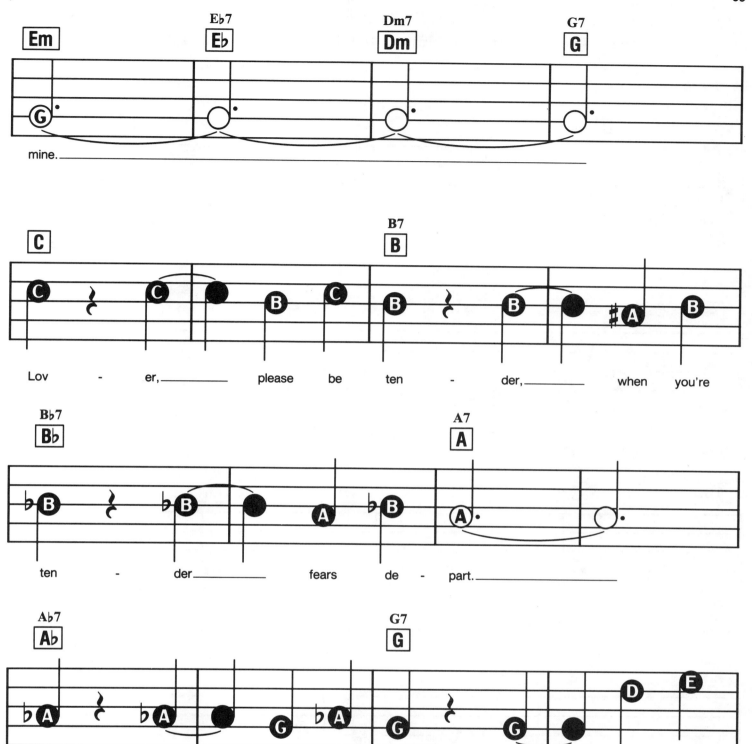

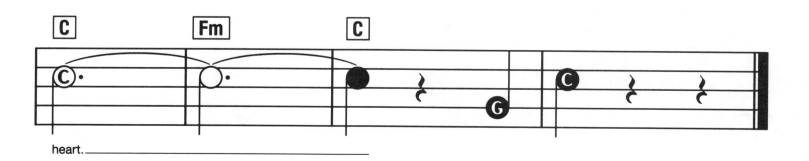

Moon River

from the Paramount Picture BREAKFAST AT TIFFANY'S

Registration 3
Rhythm: Waltz

Words by Johnny Mercer
Music by Henry Mancini

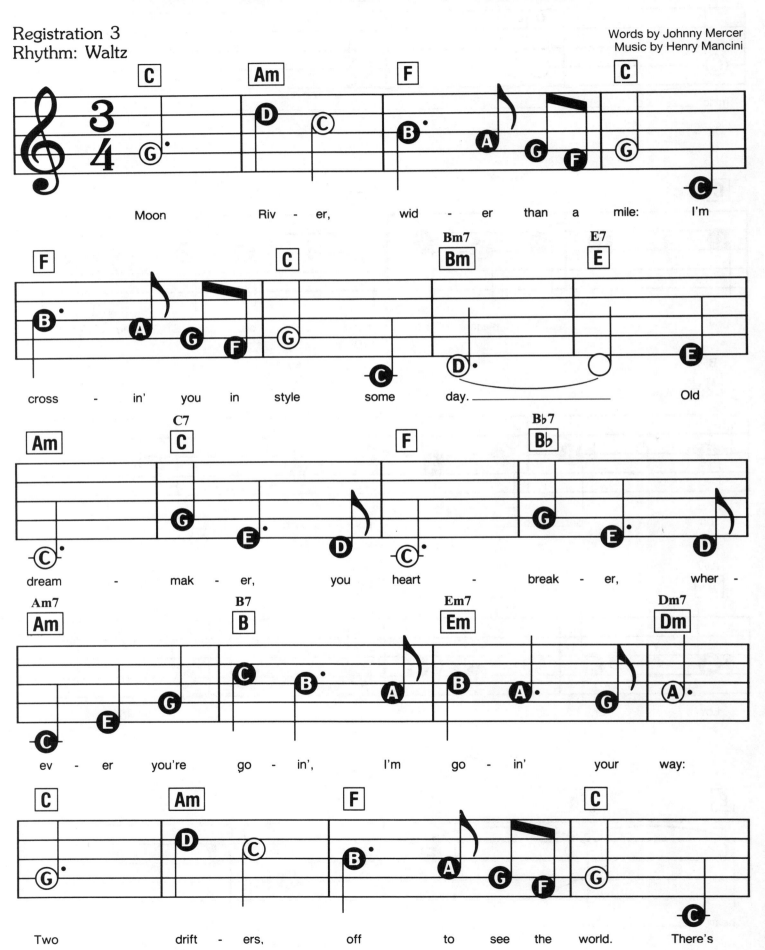

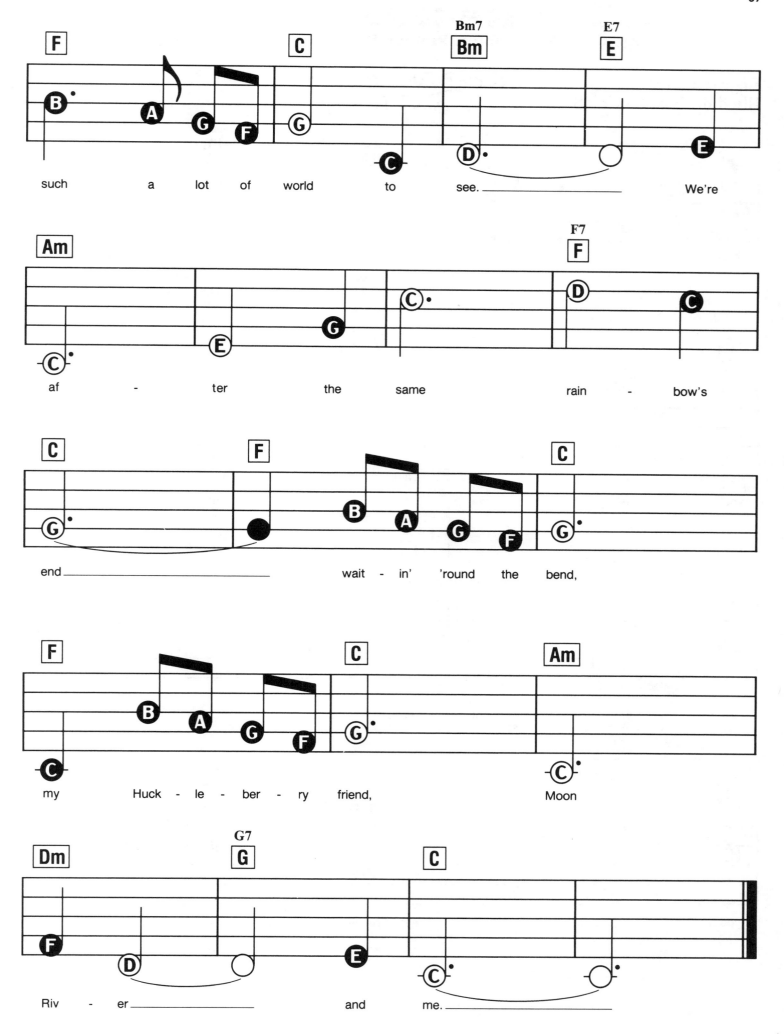

The Nearness of You
from the Paramount Picture ROMANCE IN THE DARK

Registration 9
Rhythm: Fox Trot or Swing

Words by Ned Washington
Music by Hoagy Carmichael

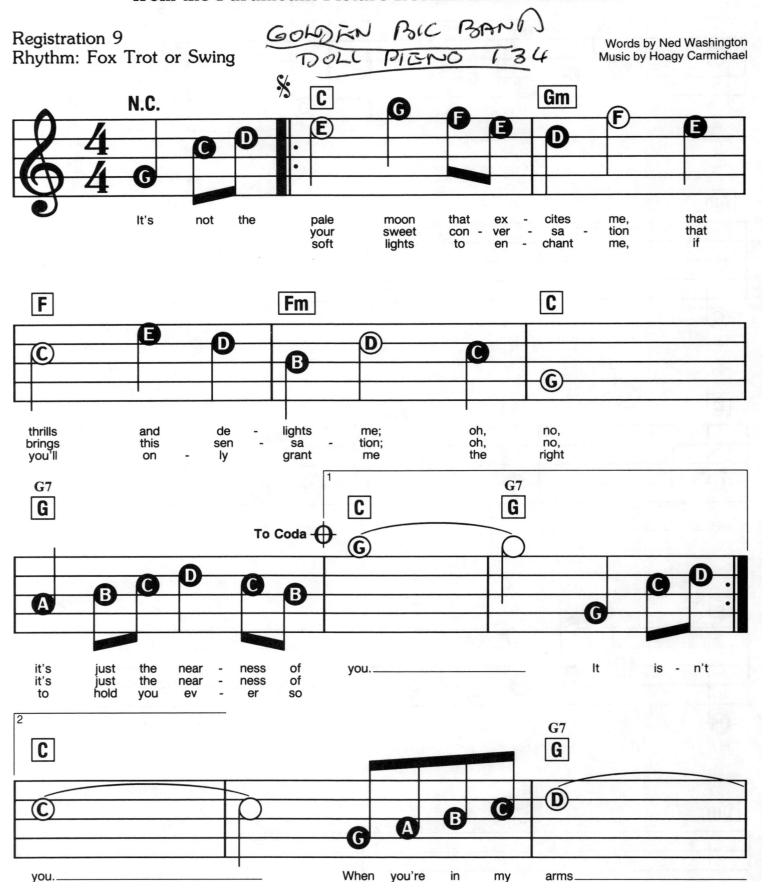

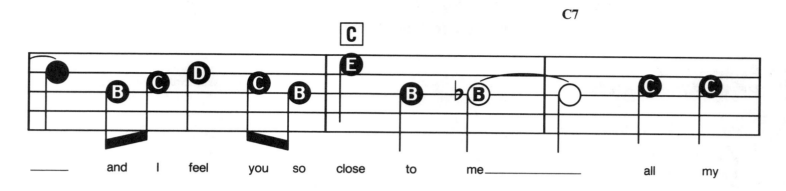

and I feel you so close to me _____ all my

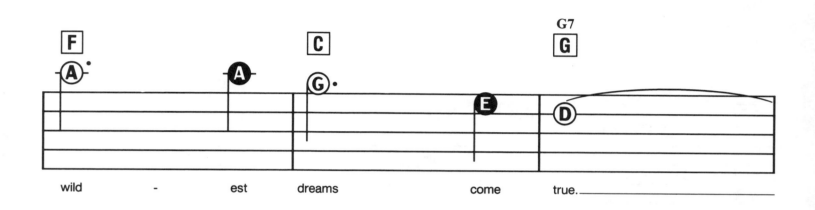

wild - est dreams come true. _____

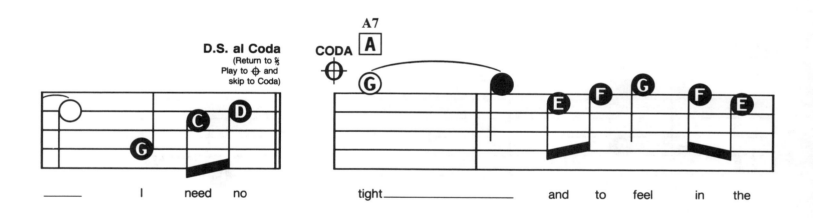

_____ I need no   tight _____ and to feel in the

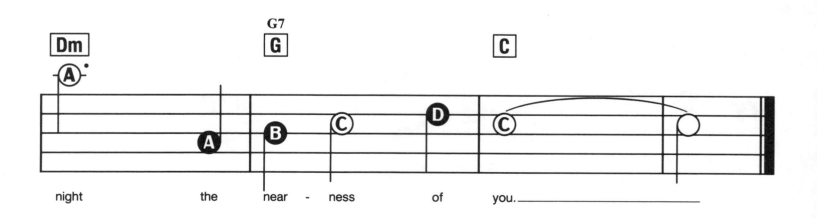

night   the near - ness of you. _____

Somewhere Out There
from AN AMERICAN TAIL

Registration 4
Rhythm: Rock or 8 Beat

Words and Music by James Horner,
Barry Mann and Cynthia Weil

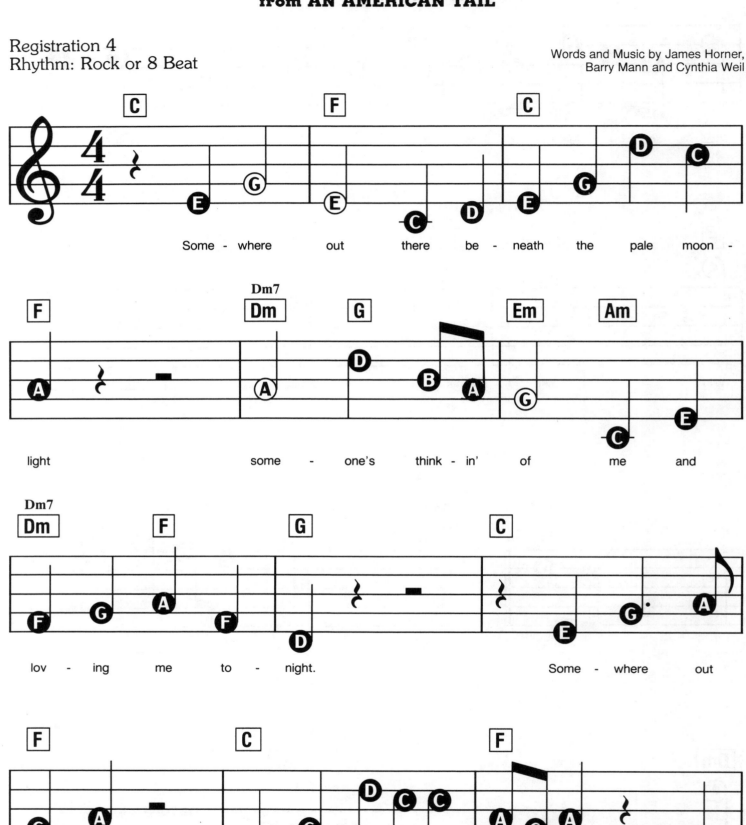

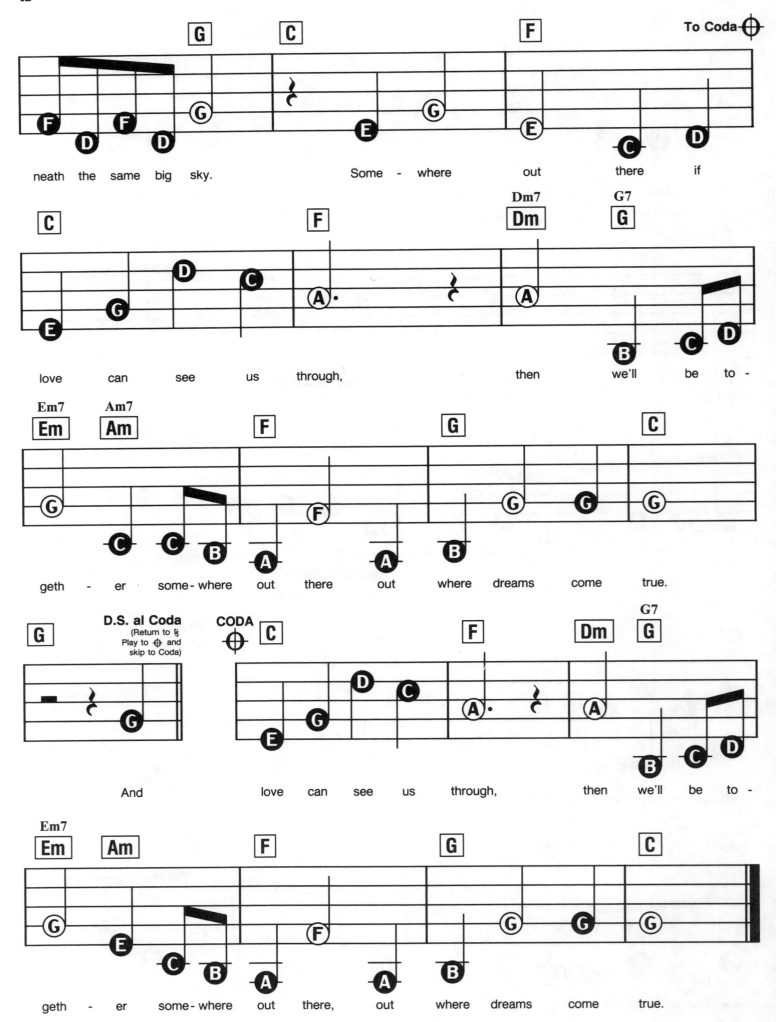

Up Where We Belong
from the Paramount Picture AN OFFICER AND A GENTLEMAN

Registration 10
Rhythm: Rock

Words by Will Jennings
Music by Jack Nitzsche and Buffy Sainte-Marie

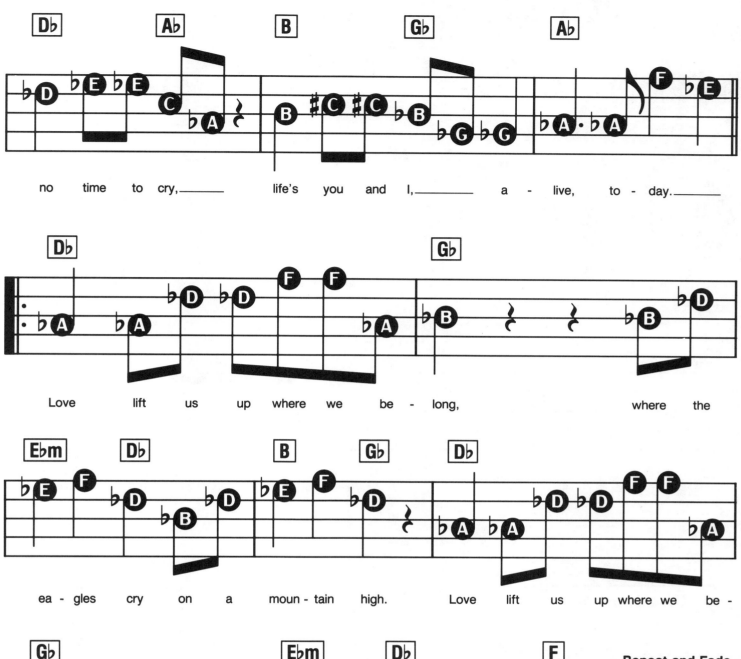

no time to cry,_____ life's you and I,_____ a - live, to - day._____

Love lift us up where we be - long, where the

ea - gles cry on a moun - tain high. Love lift us up where we be -

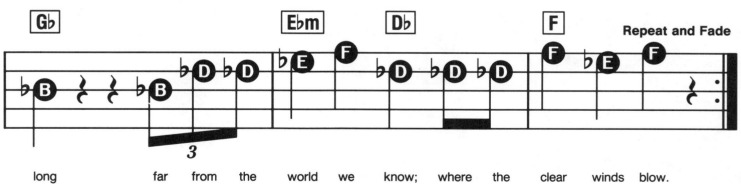

long far from the world we know; where the clear winds blow.

Additional Lyrics

2. Some hang on to "used to be,"
Live their lives looking behind.
All we have is here and now;
All our life, out there to find.
The road is long.
There are mountains in our way,
But we climb them a step every day.

Take My Breath Away
(Love Theme)
from the Paramount Picture TOP GUN

Registration 2
Rhythm: Rock or 8 Beat

Words and Music by Giorgio Moroder
and Tom Whitlock

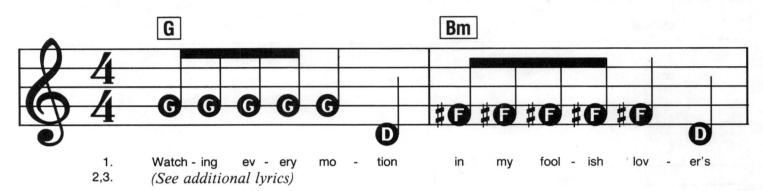

1. Watch - ing ev - ery mo - tion in my fool - ish lov - er's
2,3. *(See additional lyrics)*

game;   on this end - less o - cean,

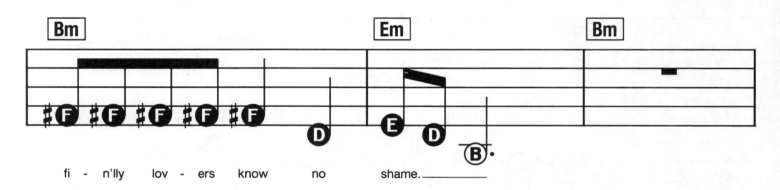

fi - n'lly lov - ers know no shame._____

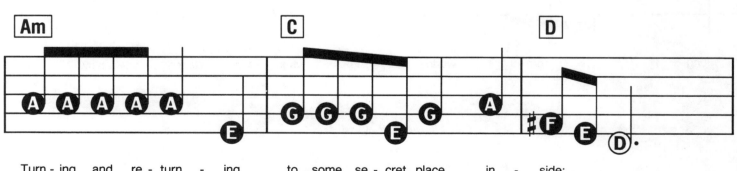

Turn - ing and re - turn - ing to some se - cret place in - side;_____

Watch - ing in slow mo - tion as you turn a - round and

say,_____ "Take my breath a - way."

"Take my breath a -

way."

Through the hour - glass I

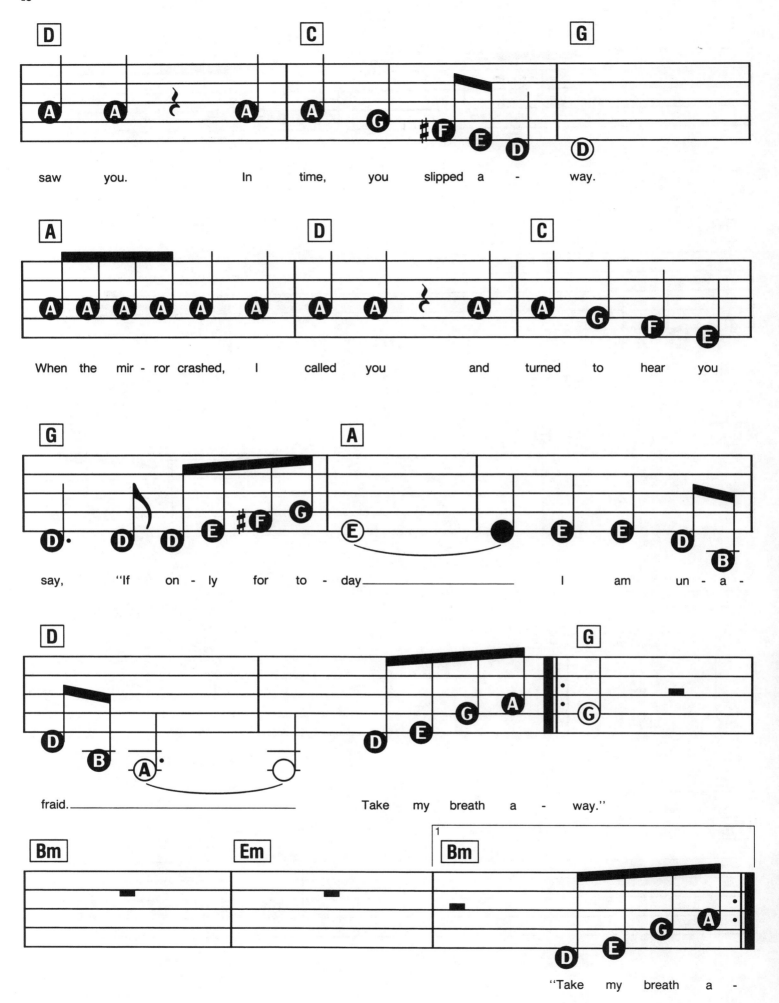

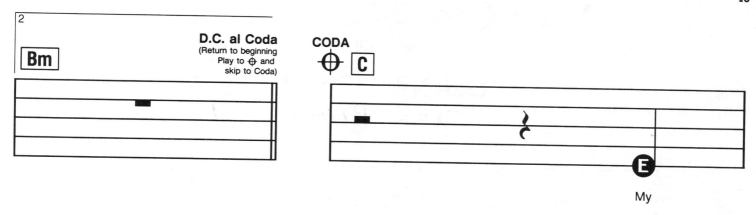

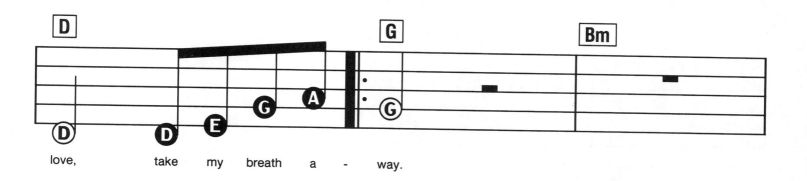

love, take my breath a - way.

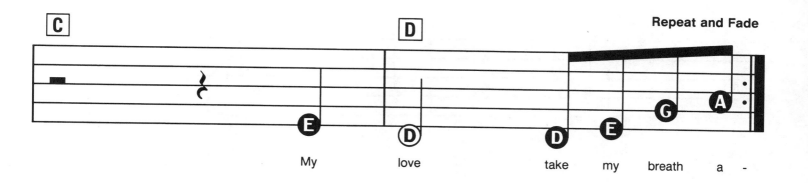

My love take my breath a -

Additional Lyrics

Verse 2:

Watching, I keep waiting, still anticipating love,
Never hesitating to become the fated ones.
Turning and returning to some secret place to hide;
Watching in slow motion as you turn my way and say,
''Take my breath away.''

Verse 3:

Watching every motion in this foolish lover's game;
Haunted by the notion somewhere there's a love in flames.
Turning and returning to some secret place inside;
Watching in slow motion as you turn to me and say,
''Take my breath away.''

That Old Black Magic

from the Paramount Picture STAR SPANGLED RHYTHM

Registration 1
Rhythm: Fox Trot or Swing

GOLDEN BIG BAND
DOLL PIANO 134

Words by Johnny Mercer
Music by Harold Arlen

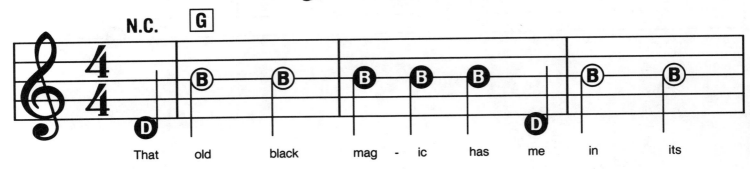

That old black mag - ic has me in its

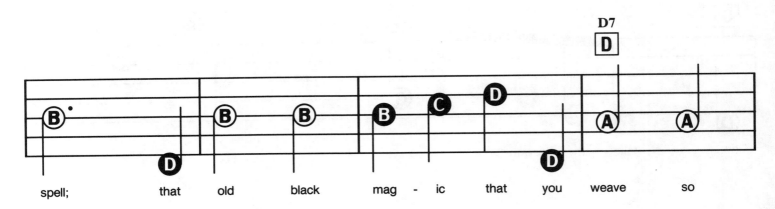

spell; that old black mag - ic that you weave so

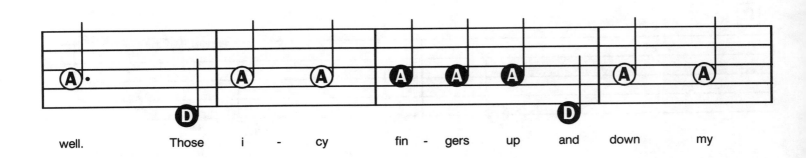

well. Those i - cy fin - gers up and down my

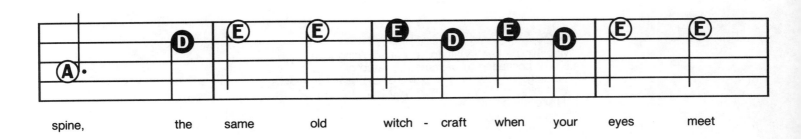

spine, the same old witch - craft when your eyes meet

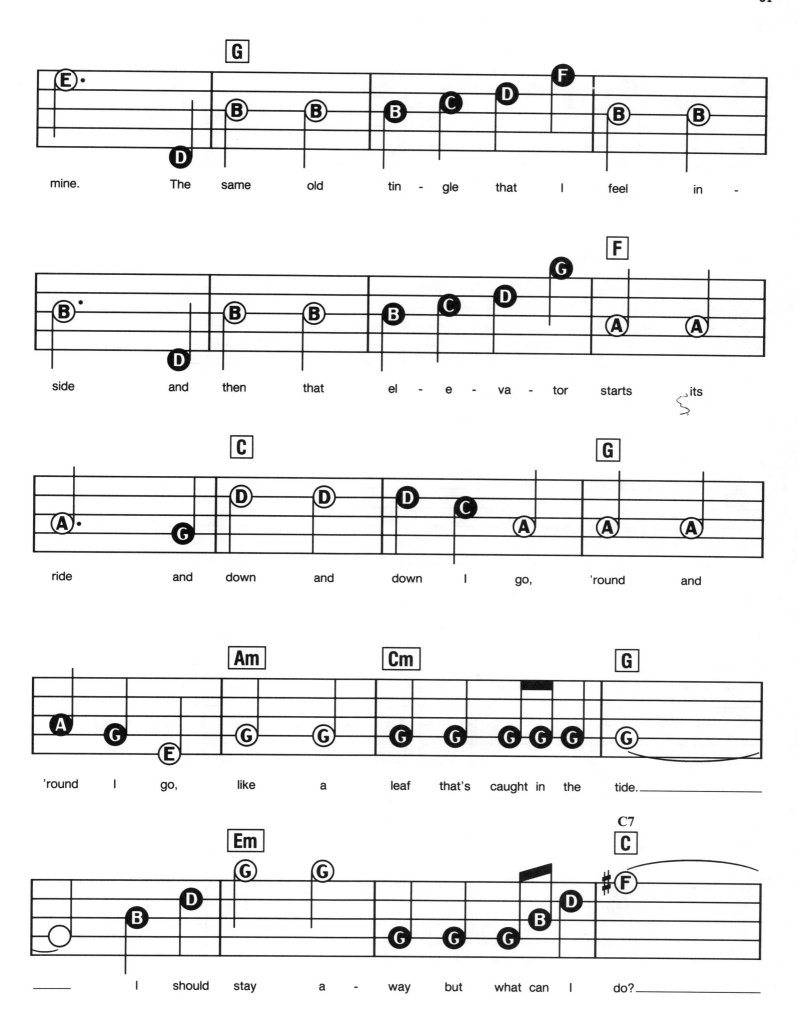

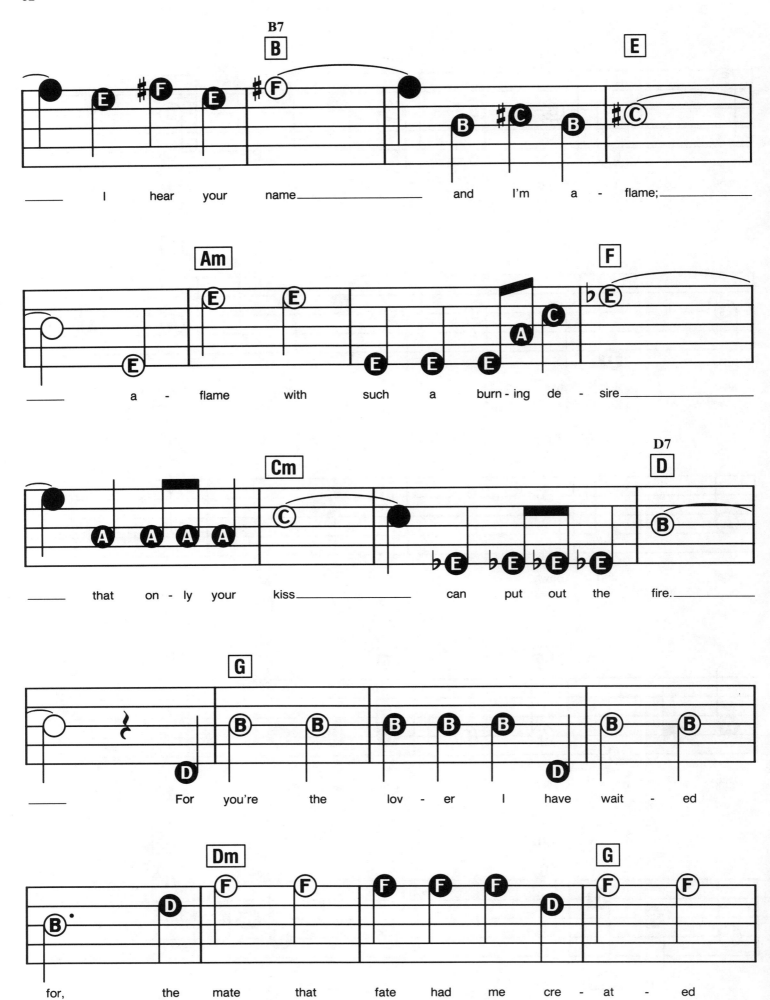

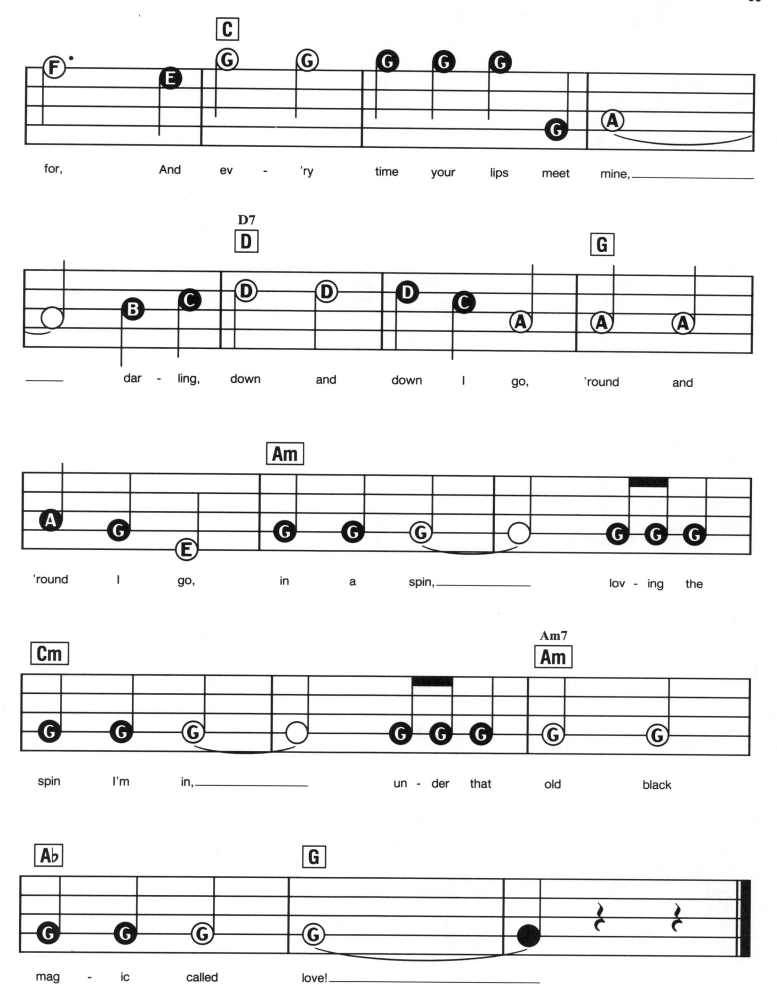

The Way You Look Tonight
from SWING TIME

Registration 3
Rhythm: Fox Trot or Swing

Words by Dorothy Fields
Music by Jerome Kern

Some — day when I'm aw - f'ly low,
2,3 love - ly, with your smile so warm

When the world is cold, I will feel a glow just think - ing
And your world cheek so soft, There is noth - ing for me but to

of you And the way you look to
love you Just the way you look to

night. Oh but you're

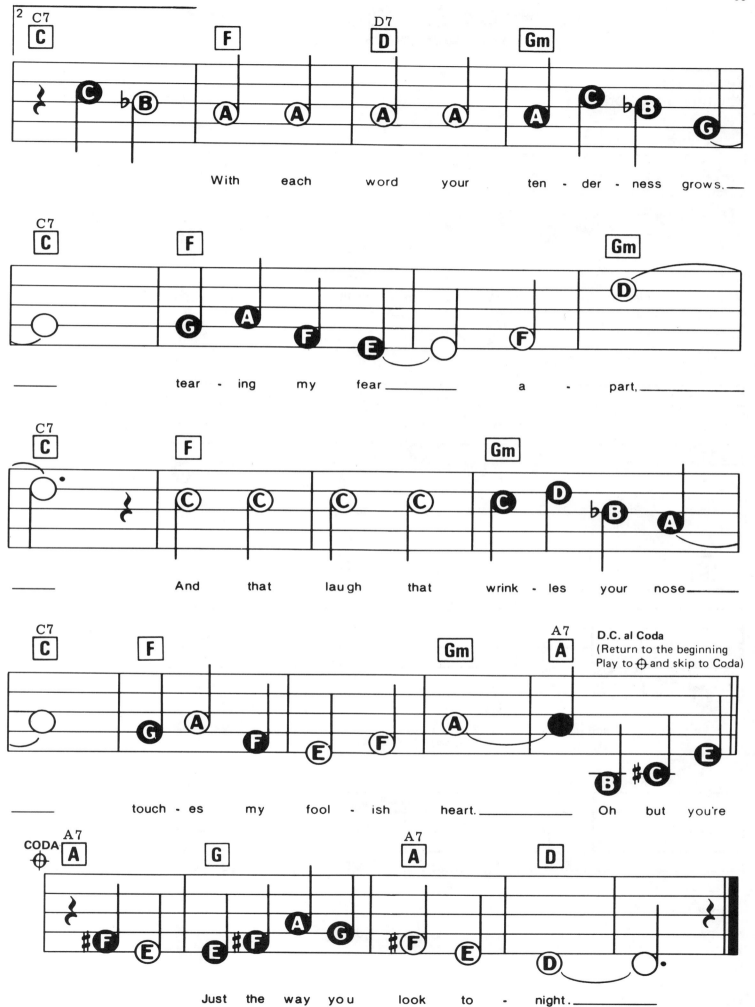

A Whole New World
from Walt Disney's ALADDIN

Registration 1
Rhythm: 8-beat or Pops

Music by Alan Menken
Lyrics by Tim Rice

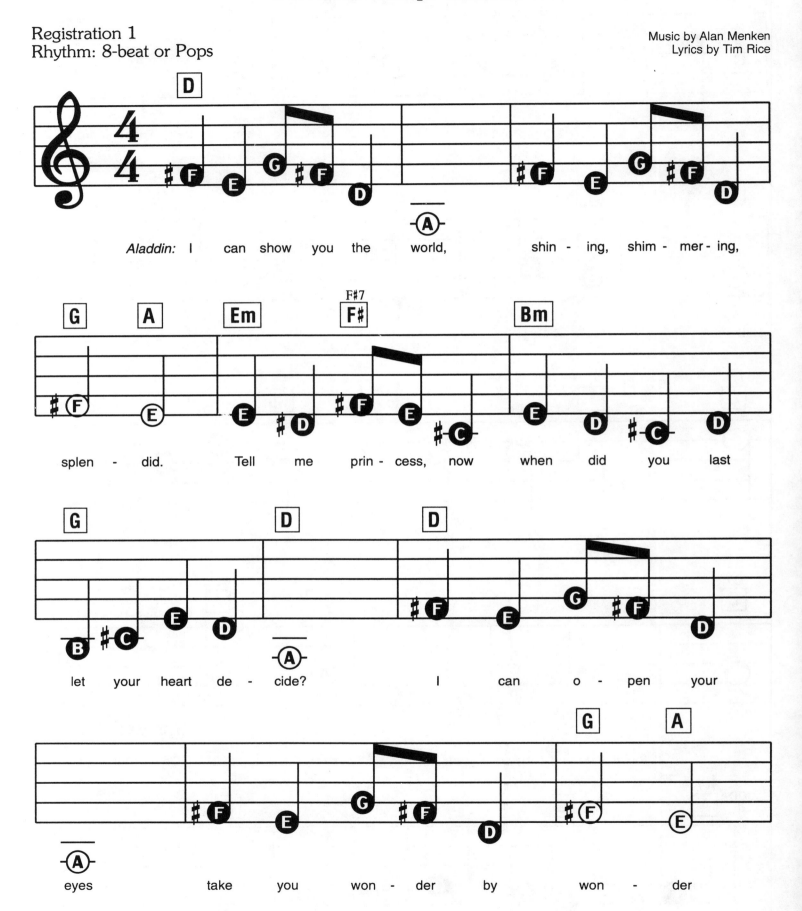

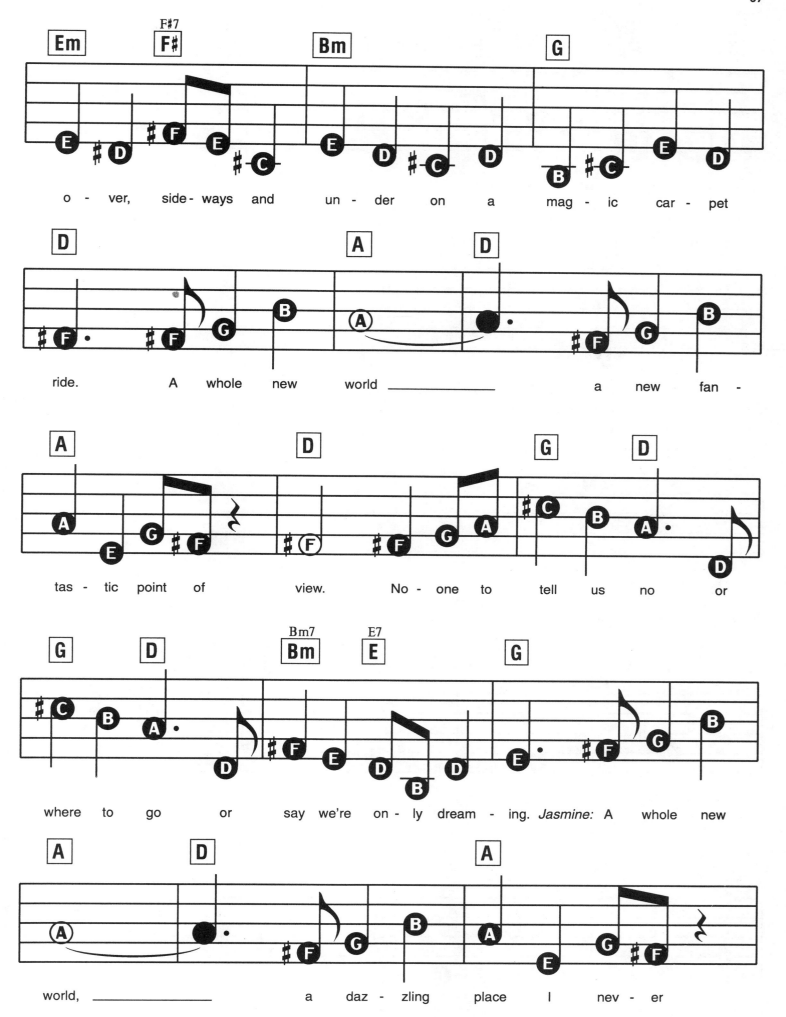

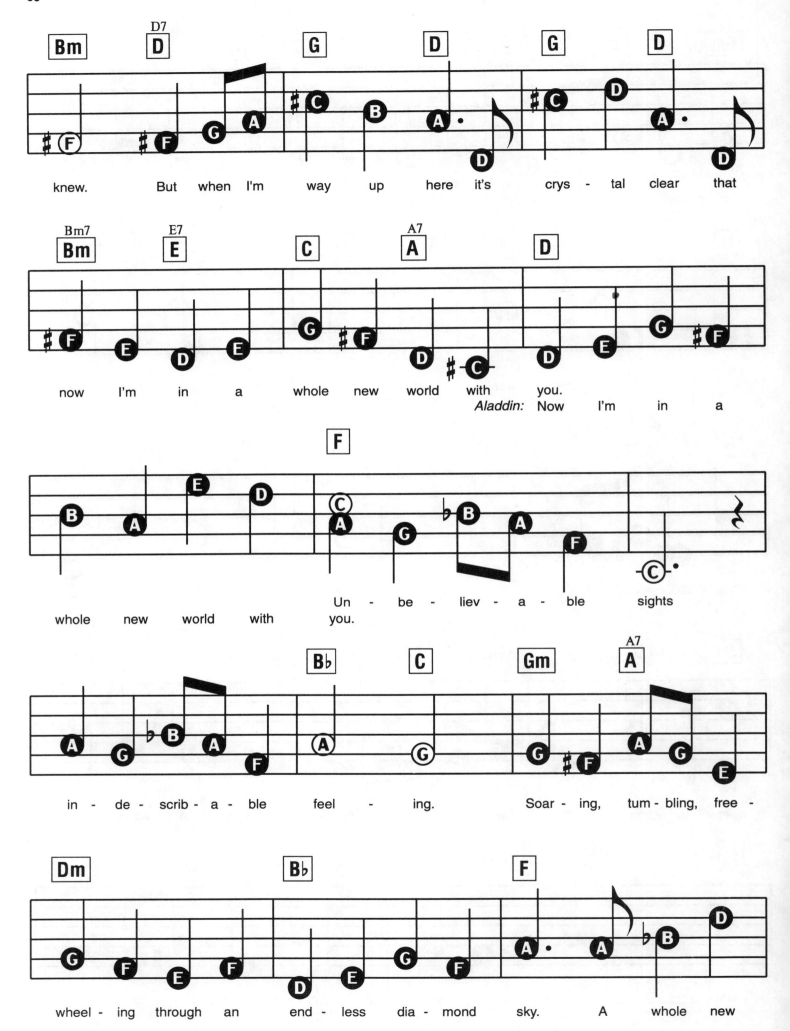

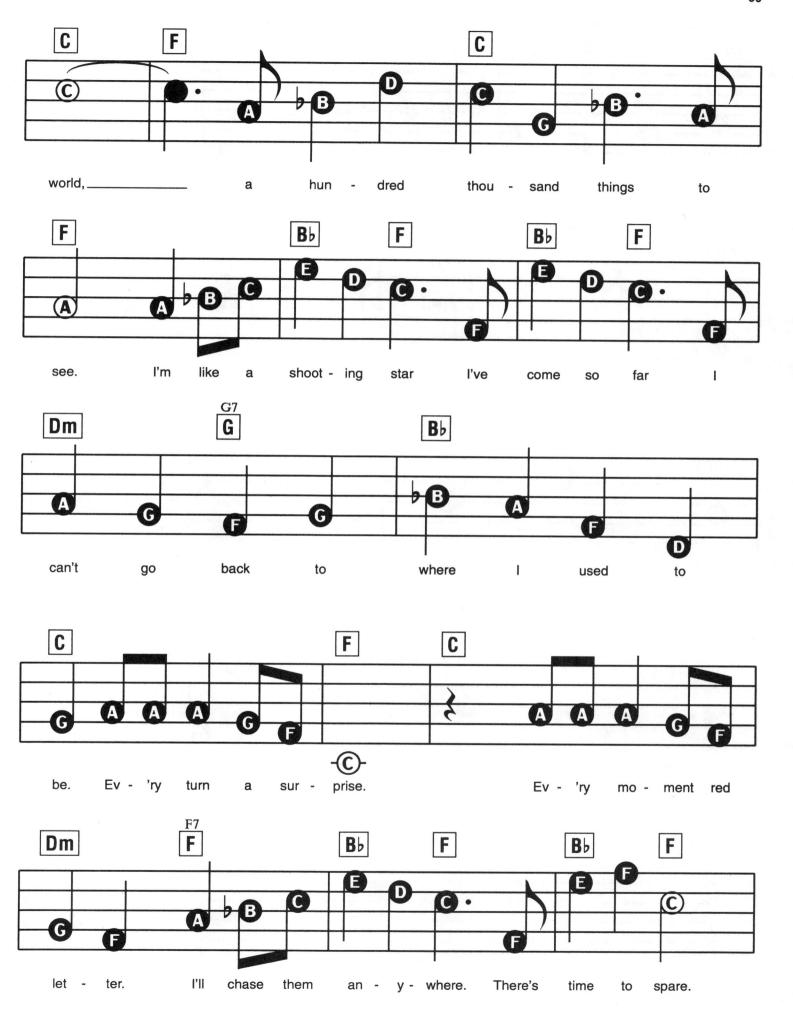

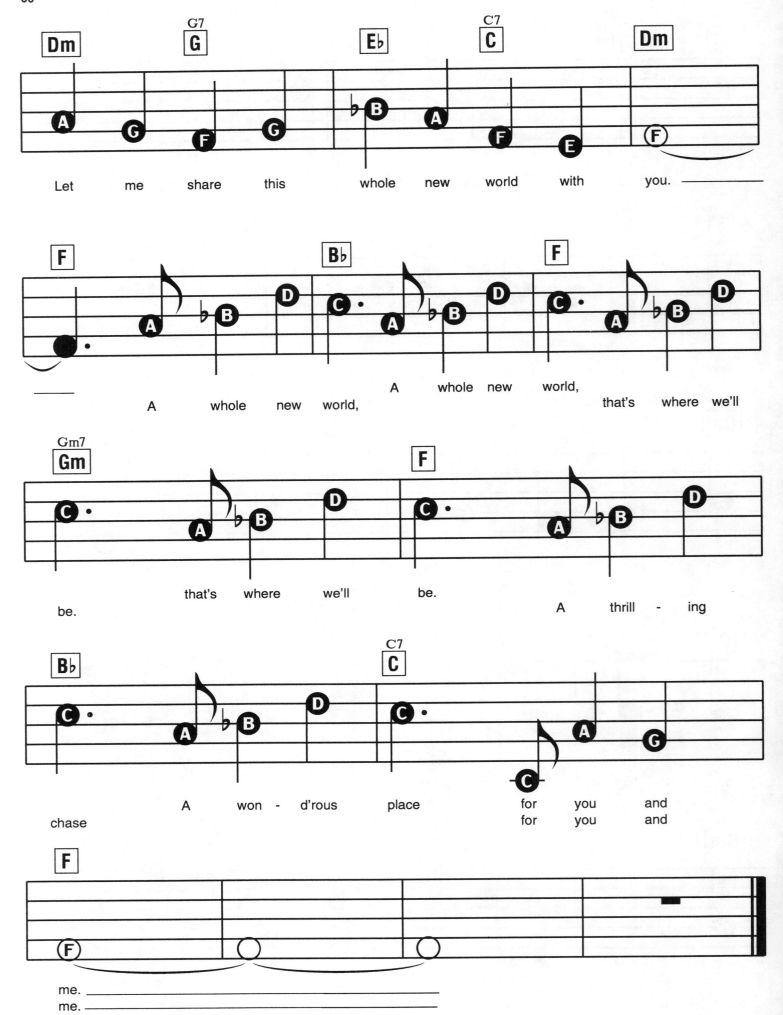

Let me share this whole new world with you. _____

_____ A whole new world, A whole new world, that's where we'll

that's where we'll be. be. A thrill - ing

A won - d'rous place for you and
chase for you and

me. _____
me. _____

You Should Be Dancing
from SATURDAY NIGHT FEVER

Registration 1
Rhythm: Disco

Words and Music by Barry Gibb,
Maurice Gibb and Robin Gibb

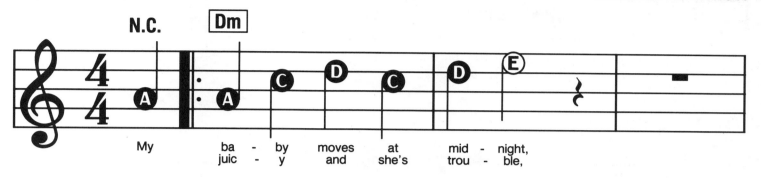

My ba - by moves at mid - night,
juic - y moves and she's trou - ble,

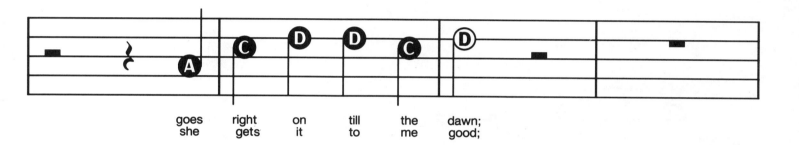

goes right on till the dawn;
she gets it to me good;

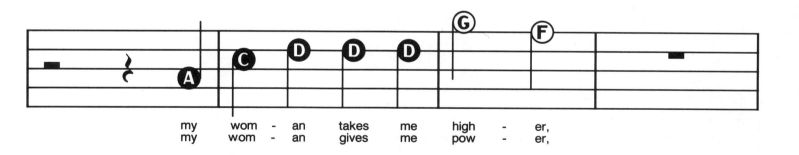

my wom - an takes me high - er,
my wom - an gives me pow - er,

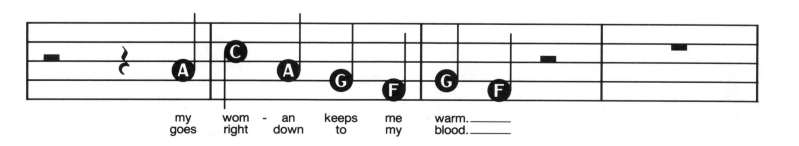

my wom - an keeps me warm.____
goes right down to my blood.____

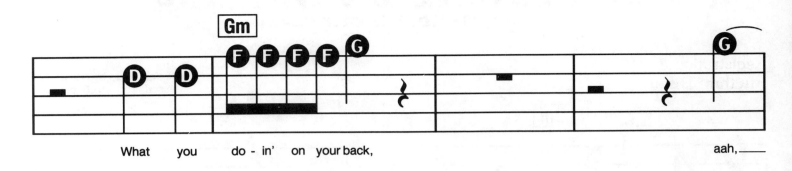

What you do - in' on your back, aah, _____

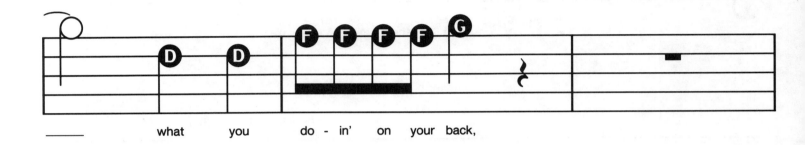

_____ what you do - in' on your back,

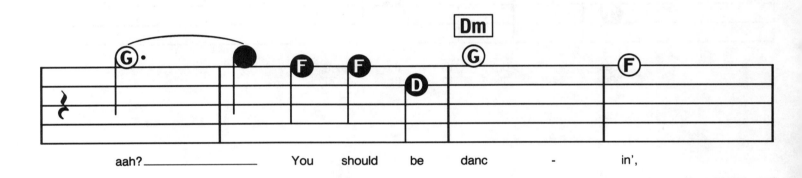

aah? _____ You should be danc - in',

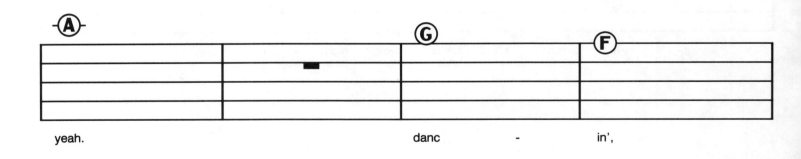

yeah. danc - in',

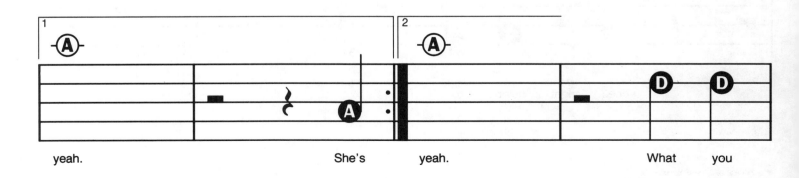

yeah. She's yeah. What you

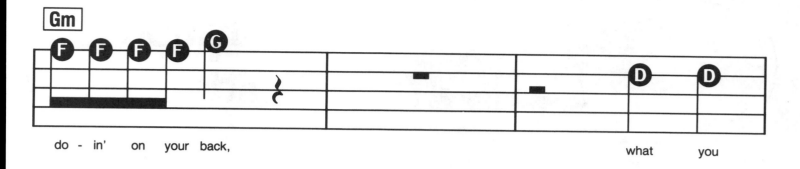

do - in' on your back,   what   you

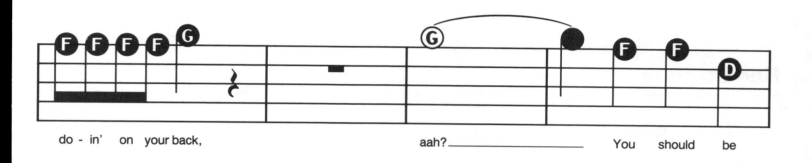

do - in'   on your back,   aah?_____ You   should   be

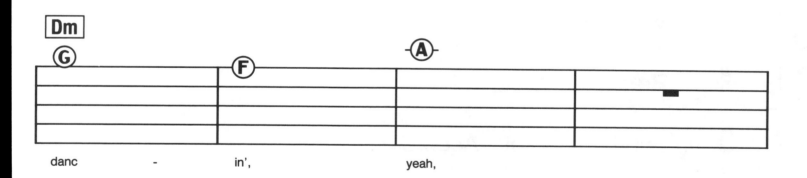

danc   -   in',   yeah,

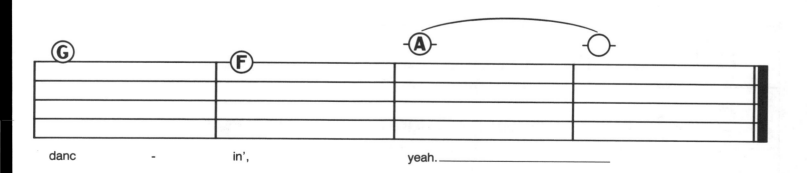

danc   -   in',   yeah._____

Registration Guide

- Match the Registration number on the song to the corresponding numbered category below. Select and activate an instrumental sound available on your instrument.

- Choose an automatic rhythm appropriate to the mood and style of the song. (Consult your Owner's Guide for proper operation of automatic rhythm features.)

- Adjust the tempo and volume controls to comfortable settings.

Registration

1	Flute, Pan Flute, Jazz Flute
2	Clarinet, Organ
3	Violin, Strings
4	Brass, Trumpet
5	Synth Ensemble, Accordion, Brass
6	Pipe Organ, Harpsichord
7	Jazz Organ, Vibraphone, Vibes, Electric Piano, Jazz Guitar
8	Piano, Electric Piano
9	Trumpet, Trombone, Clarinet, Saxophone, Oboe
10	Violin, Cello, Strings